THE EXPAT'S GUIDE TO BUYING REAL ESTATE IN ITALY

BY

BRAD ALLAN

Copyright © 2024 by Brad Allan

All rights reserved. No part of this publication may be reproduced, distributed, or transmitted in any form or by any means, including photocopying, recording, or other electronic or mechanical methods, without the prior written permission of the publisher, except in the case of brief quotations embodied in critical reviews and certain other noncommercial uses permitted by copyright law.

This book is not intended to give legal, accounting or investment advice. Please seek out professionals in those fields for the current laws and best practices.

For permission requests, write to the publisher via email at: brad@BradsWorld.it

www.BradsWorld.it

2nd Edition

PREFACE

For years I dreamed about moving to Italy. During the covid pandemic, I decided to solidify my plans and make the financial moves necessary to permanently move to Italy *well* before retirement age. It is the cost of living in Italy that will allow you to live a more fulfilling life regardless of your age. Whether you are retiring, working remotely, or just taking a few years off to enjoy life, you have made the right decision looking into Italy.

I knew that moving to Italy, learning a new language in my 50's, and trying to understand whole new systems of government, healthcare, and personal interactions would be difficult. However, I found that most people here are very accepting and go out of their way to help you. I practiced my Italian and today can communicate in my new country's language. This is the most important thing you can do… Learn the Italian language!

I also found I wanted to help people like myself who are looking for answers, so I started my YouTube channel **BradsWorld** in 2022. This book is a companion to my YouTube Channel. BradsWorld has put me in contact with hundreds of people around the world with so many questions that needed answering. I hope this book and my videos on BradsWorld are helpful to all and I appreciate the friendships I have formed from starting this journey!

BRAD ALLAN
Tuscany, Italy
January 2024

TABLE OF CONTENTS

Introduction   6
    Importance of understanding the Italian real estate market
    Considerations for making Italian property purchases

Understanding the Italian Real Estate Market   21
    Overview of Italian Real Estate Market Today

Legal and Regulatory Landscape   28
    Overview of the legal system in Italy
    Key Legal Requirements for Expats
    Legal Process for Property Transactions

Financing Your Home Purchase   42
    Financing Options for Expats
    Overview of Mortgage Process in Italy

Types of Homes to Buy   49
    Villas, Historic Centers, and Modern Homes
    Inexpensive Apartments and Homes
    €1 Homes Explained

Working with Italian Real Estate Agents   57
    Importance Considerations for Choosing Agents
    Benefits of Working with Real Estate Agents
    Challenges and Considerations

Tax Implications   65
    Overview of property taxes in Italy
    Tax considerations for expats

Maintenance and Renovations   71
    Understanding property maintenance in Italy
    Finding reliable contractors and suppliers

Best Cities and Areas for Expats in Italy

Lake Como	**81**
Turin	**88**
Milan	**94**
Verona	**101**
Treviso	**107**
Venice	**114**
Lucca	**123**
Pisa	**130**
Florence	**134**
San Gimignano	**140**
Montepulciano	**144**
Siena	**150**
Perugia	**155**
Todi	**160**
Orvieto	**167**
Rome	**173**
Naples	**184**
Lecce	**194**

Geographic Areas:

Sicily	**201**
Sardinia	**212**
Frosinone	**222**

Chapter 1

INTRODUCTION

IMPORTANCE OF UNDERSTANDING THE ITALIAN REAL ESTATE MARKET

Even after purchasing over 200 individual apartments and more than 20 investment homes in the United States between 2000 and 2022, I felt very lost when it came time for me to start getting serious about looking for properties in the country I had come to love through my travels here for two decades. I had no idea where to start with understanding market values in particular places. Would I buy in Lucca, or San Gimignano, or Montepulciano? Would I try to renovate one of the great old farmhouses that had fallen into disrepair or buy something that had all the hard work done to it already? Who was going to help me with all of these things and how would I NOT fall prey to shysters and charlatans who would inevitably prey on a newbie like myself.

First, let me start by saying that Italy is a gigantic real estate market with hundreds of thousands of listings. Each area is very unique from the next and prices can vary 500% within just a few kilometres. I talk all the time on my YouTube channel, BradsWorld, about the importance of spending time in whatever market you're seriously looking at. You'll hear this refrain again and again in my book, "if you don't have the time to spend weeks or even months living, experiencing, and researching your target areas, it's probably not time for you to be thinking about buying an investment property or a personal home here".

A thorough understanding of the various regions of Italy goes along way to helping you decide where to focus your search for your next investment property or your forever home. It's not necessary to go just to Southern Italy to find something that's very reasonable... inexpensive properties can be found throughout Italy. Even in high traffic tourist areas like Tuscany, it's still possible to find an independent home for well under €100,000 that is move-in ready. Apartments can be had for €30,000 that are near all services including major medical.

Really what you're looking for in the different regions is the lifestyle and cultural differences that each region can offer. Do you want to be in Southern Italy where it could be very hot and there's ample sandy beaches? Or do you wanna be in northern Italy where there's winter sports and great hiking and a more refined way of living?

The Italian real estate market has historically been influenced by economic, social, and political factors. Italy's economic stability, or lack thereof, plays a pivotal role in determining property prices. By keeping a keen eye on economic indicators and trends, expats can make informed decisions about when and where to invest. For instance, I bought all of my properties here when the Euro crashed against the dollar during the pandemic in 2021 and 2022. I was able to get a 17% discount on my remodelling just because of the timing of when I had to send the funds to pay for everything. And for the record, it was partly luck. Being able to track and take a good educated guess about when is the best time to move on a property or to simply figure out when to wire transfer you money can make a huge difference.

Legal intricacies add another layer of complexity to the Italian real estate market. The legal framework governing property ownership and transactions can be notably different from what expats may be accustomed to in their home countries. An understanding of Italian property laws and regulations is not only necessary to navigate the buying process smoothly but also to ensure a secure and legally sound investment.

The charm of Italy often lies in its historical properties, from ancient villas to renovated farmhouses. However, these properties come with their own set of challenges, including maintenance costs, preservation regulations, and potential unforeseen issues. Like a lot of people I spent many 100's of hours online during covid looking at and dreaming about buying some neat old property and working to transform it into something special. But while you are looking at the properties themselves, make sure you are checking into the costs of all the things you will need to make your property a winner.

You also need to begin TODAY learning the Italian language. Nobody here expects you to be able to be fluent. The reality is you will probably never become fluent in the language. But it is important for many different reasons to be able to speak *some* Italian. Outside of major tourists areas the amount of English or other foreign languages spoken drops off to a small percentage of residents. You can get by with your google translate, but it isn't foolproof and sometimes there is no cell service and then what do you do? You need to be able to speak some Italian to be able to forge new friendships. Speak their language is simple respectful and the right thing to do.

I spent over 1500 hours on Duolingo and HelloTalk, two apps that you can find for any type of cellphone that are really great ways to pick up the basics (or more) of Italian.

Duolingo teaches the basics of grammar and a lot of important words to know for everyday conversation. It will take you about 12-18 months to get through the entire program if you are diligent and study every day. The total cost for that is around $100. A very small investment for such an important part of what will make your new life in Italy satisfying.

HelloTalk is a lesser-known app that pairs people in different countries together that are looking to learn each other's language. You can form friendships with people and it makes communicating fun. Even though I haven't used the app for over two years, I'm still in touch with a number of the people that I was studying with. My one friend, Serena, who was between jobs at the time, would listen to me read *Alice in Wonderland* in Italian every day by FaceTime to help me with my pronunciation. To this day people say that I have very good pronunciation in Italian and that is why!

Financing options further underscore the importance of understanding the Italian real estate market. When I first started looking into seriously buying a place in Italy, it was possible for an expat to get a loan from an Italian bank at under 2% ARM, for 20 years, with 30% down. Then the war in Ukraine broke out and banks pulled back from lending to foreigners. Fast forward 3 years and it is still very difficult for foreigners to get a loan from Italian banks, but once you have your residency you should be able to procure a loan with good rates from a local bank if you have a working relationship with them. If you don't have your residency or dual citizenship, you'll find it it's virtually impossible to get a loan from an Italian bank on an Italian property.

Location is key in the Italian real estate market, and expats must carefully choose where to invest based on their preferences, lifestyle, and potential for property appreciation. Whether it's the romantic canals of Venice, the scenic allure of Tuscany, or the sun-soaked landscapes of Sicily, each location carries its unique advantages and considerations. Knowing the pulse of different regions enables expats to align their investment with their personal and financial goals.

Understanding the Italian real estate market is not just a matter of due diligence; it is a gateway to a successful and fulfilling expat experience. From navigating legal complexities to seizing strategic investment opportunities, a comprehensive understanding of the Italian real estate market empowers expatriates to make informed decisions that resonate with their aspirations and contribute to a seamless integration into the Italian way of life. The rewards of such understanding extend far beyond the transaction itself, enriching the expat journey with the timeless allure of "la dolce vita".

CONSIDERATIONS FOR EXPATS MAKING PROPERTY PURCHASES IN ITALY

Italy, with its rich history and stunning landscapes, has long been a dream destination for expatriates seeking to make this enchanting country their home. For those considering the significant step of buying property in Italy, navigating the complexities of the real estate market requires a deep understanding of various aspects. Let's take a quick look at the crucial elements that expats must consider to ensure a smooth and rewarding experience on their Italian property journey.

Legal and Regulatory Landscape

If Law and financial items confuse you at home get ready to have your mind blown away when you arrive in Italy. I always considered myself to be of above average intelligence and after 20 years doing commercial real estate deals in the United States I thought I had seen and learned most everything. Doing business and the structure of deals in Italy is more than likely very different than anything you've ever experienced in the past.

Navigating Italian bureaucracy can be intricate and overwhelming, but with the right professional help expats can avoid pitfalls and ensure a smooth transition from property search to ownership. Engaging a local legal expert can be invaluable in providing guidance through the complexities of Italian property law. There are many lawyers and accountants that practice simultaneously in the United States and in Italy who can help bridge the gaps you may have in your knowledge.

As I said earlier, you're investing more than likely a large chunk of your nest egg into buying a property here in Italy. You cannot afford to make a mistake that will leave you open to claims in the future on the property. Again, the laws are very arcane and based on Roman law. I've heard stories of people having distant relatives of the person they bought their house from come and make a claim on the purchase against the property years later!

Financial Considerations

Financing a property purchase in Italy involves understanding the financial aspects unique to the country. Expats should be well-versed in mortgage processes, interest rates, and financing options available. I came to Italy personally with liquidity to buy multiple income properties using only cash. I have a long history of doing deals and in investment or commercial property, leverage is key to being able to make outsized profits versus paying only cash. In the end, all the promises I had to be able to get financing on property purchases before I was a resident vanished into thin air. Now that I have my residency finalised I can now get very favorable terms from the local banks to buy a home here. That residency process can take up to a year and if you are moving here to get residency you are going to need to show a lease or a deed for property where you can stay for the first 12 months. These "Catch-22's" are emblematic of all the problems you will encounter when relocating to Italy. But remember, they are all surmountable!

Budgeting is a key aspect, and expats should not only consider the property's purchase price but also factor in additional costs such as property taxes (transfer taxes at closing are highest), notary fees (will be 1000's of dollars/euros/whatever…), and potential renovation expenses. Agent fees for the buyers agent are paid by the buyers themselves, so you need to figure that usually 3% fee into your calculations. Again remember that if you are buying a low cost home or apt it will still be $3,000+- owed to the agent for seeing the purchase through. Being financially prepared ensures a realistic and sustainable investment in the Italian real estate market.

Choosing the Right Location

Italy boasts a diverse range of regions, each with its own distinct charm and lifestyle. Expats should carefully consider their preferences and needs when choosing the location for their property. I had traveled extensively in Italy for almost 2 decades. That helped me narrow down my choice to just a handful of regions. But even just a couple regions gives you many thousands of square kilometres each to choose from, each area having its own peculiarities that make it special.

Proximity to amenities, transportation, and medical care are crucial factors. Medical care and the availability of a top tier hospital should be the number one thing that you are interested in being close to. Forget about which beach the house is nearest too, think about which hospital has life flight capabilities, and which specialists are in the area. The medical system in Italy can be top-notch for preventative care and if you're becoming a resident here you're going to be taken into the system. It was the number one reason that my wife and I decided to make the moved Italy. The fact that she's a cancer survivor and needs ongoing screening was a perfect fit for the Italian system. She is being taken into a program that will give her full work ups and scans every six months free of charge. In the United States we were paying almost $1500 a month just for medical insurance since we were self-employed. This is just one of the huge savings we experience by moving to Italy versus the United States.

Understanding the local infrastructure and community dynamics helps expats make informed decisions about the location that aligns with their lifestyle and long-term goals. While it can be enticing to think about moving to the southern part of Italy for the lower tax rates and for cheaper housing, ex-pats, and especially retirees should carefully consider the availability of good medical care and overall services.

Types of Properties

The Italian real estate market offers a variety of property types, ranging from historic villas to modern apartments. Expats need to consider their preferences, lifestyle, and future plans when selecting a property type. Historical properties may come with unique charm but also maintenance challenges, while modern constructions offer convenience but may lack the character of older homes.

Understanding the pros and cons of different property types is essential for making a choice that suits the expat's preferences and aligns with their vision of the ideal Italian home.

Working with Real Estate Agents

Engaging a reliable local real estate agent is a crucial step in the property buying process. A knowledgeable agent can provide valuable insights into the local market, help identify suitable properties, and guide expats through the negotiation and purchasing processes.

Expats should take the time to research and choose an agent with a solid reputation, ensuring transparency, professionalism, and effective communication. Building a trusting relationship with a local real estate expert can significantly ease the complexities of buying property in Italy. If you are not fluent in Italian, it is advised that you work with an agency or agent that is at the very least conversational in your home language. Buying a property in Italy is convoluted enough without the added burden of trying to work solely through translation apps with your agent.

Buyers should be aware that in Italy, the buyer pays the buyers agent and the seller pays the sellers agent if there is one. It is important that you have great representation from your agent. Italian agents will normally give you a lot of services after the sale as well like helping to transfer the services on the property or perhaps finding contractors to help with remodelling. Be prepared for the fact that buying a property in Italy is very different than in some other countries. There is no MLS (Multiple Listing Service) for example like the United States has. This centralised listing service is indispensable when looking for a home as it has all the information in one spot, plus information on taxes, schools and more. Italy in comparison has no such thing, and listing services tend to show the same houses over and over from different agencies because the listings are often pirated and the information is not the same in each listing. Listings in Italy also tend to stay on the listing services well after the property is sold. The reason is that the listing acts as advertising for the agency so they are loathe to remove it quickly when the sale is done.

Navigating the Buying Process

Understanding the step-by-step process of buying property in Italy is fundamental for expats. From the initial property search to the final contract signing, each stage requires careful attention and diligence. A detailed knowledge of the required documentation, timelines, and potential challenges enables expats to navigate the process confidently.

It's advisable to engage a notary early in the process, as they play a crucial role in ensuring the legality of the transaction. Thorough due diligence, including property inspections and legal checks, is essential to mitigate any risks associated with the purchase.

Tax Implications

Italy has its own unique set of taxes, and expats need to be aware of the tax implications associated with property ownership. Understanding property tax rates, exemptions, and any changes in tax regulations is essential for financial planning. Later in the book we have a whole chapter dedicated to this subject. I can tell you that one bit of good news is that the one tax for purchasing that you are probably most worried about is the "Transfer Tax" that is paid at closing. It is 9% if this is not your primary full time residence, and 2% if it will be. But this percentage is not charged on the purchase price but on the cadastral value of the house as set by the local authorities. The cadastral value can be a very small percentage of the actual value or selling price of the property. I the case of my biggest purchase here, it was 16% of the actual selling price of the house! That dropped my Transfer Tax owed down by over €40.000 from what I was expecting. Your real estate agent should be able to give you exact numbers before you make a contract on what you total tax burdens will be on the property purchase.

Expats should also explore potential tax benefits and incentives that may apply to them, considering their residency status and the intended use of the property. Consulting with a tax advisor familiar with Italian regulations can help optimize the tax situation for expats. The Italian government has plans that allow you to pay a lower rate on your pension income for example if you move to some of the less desirable southern areas of Italy like Calabria and Sicily. Just be aware that there is a reason why the government here is giving away money to entice you to move to these areas.... Nothing is for free. €1 homes and tax incentives to get you to move there are sure signs of issues with the areas that you need to fully investigate before moving there.

Cultural and Social Integration

Buying property in Italy is not just a financial transaction; it's a cultural and social investment. Expats should be mindful of cultural nuances and local customs to facilitate a smooth integration into the community. Building relationships with neighbors, participating in local events, and embracing the Italian way of life contribute to a fulfilling expat experience.

Understanding the importance of family, community, and tradition in Italian culture allows expats to form meaningful connections and create a sense of belonging. If you come to Italy trying to turn it into your previous home country, you will most certainly have a difficult time transitioning into your new Italian life. Try to read up on the cultural aspects of Italian life that make it so unique. No one expects you to become Italian overnight, but if you put some work into educating yourself on life here beforehand, it will certainly pay dividends for you when you finally arrive.

Maintenance and Renovations

Property ownership comes with responsibilities, and understanding the maintenance requirements and potential renovation challenges is crucial. Historical properties, while charming, may require specialized maintenance, and adherence to preservation regulations is essential. You should always engage an architect that services your town specifically to help getting the renovations you need done passed by the local authorities. Failure to adhere to local laws regarding the renovation of historical buildings can open you up to fines or worse. But you can and should do as much of the work as possible. Prices in Italy are probably lower than what you are used to in other first world nations, but it still isn't cheap. We painted a kitchen with high ceilings in one of our apartments in about 4 hours that we had been quoted €1400 for the job. Simple afternoon and not a big deal! If you can do those kinds of savings over and over, you can take a lot of the load of making your new home or investment property liveable very quickly.

Residency and Visa Considerations

I purposely decided for this book not to go into detail about visas and the residency process. There were huge variations in the rules just among the various consulate locations in the United States for example. Some allow both couples to qualify with €40,000 income for the ERV (Elective Residency Visa) and other conflicts require each couple to have €32,000 worth of income for a total of over €60,000. It's these types of differences that can make even writing about the visa process difficult. I can tell you that we used the Houston consulate in Texas to process our visa application, and they were wonderful to work with. Our visa was done in less than a month from the day I submitted the application with all the requested documentation. We never even had an appointment, I just shipped everything to them via trackable overnight service and provided a self return trackable envelope for them to send the passports back to me. One important hit I will give you about the application process is that if you were applying as a couple for the ERV, you need to submit to complete packages as if you were single. That holds true even for joint accounts or properties that are owned in both names. If you have a joint banking account, you need to print out one years worth of activity in two complete copies and each packet gets one copy. They will treat your applications as an individual even if you were applying as a couple.

For expats intending to make Italy their primary residence, understanding residency and visa requirements is paramount. It is not a requirement to have a visa to stay in Italy for less than 90 days (every 180 days). Some people find that they enjoy living in Italy part of the year and another expat country or their home country the other part of the year.

We personally had very important reasons why we decided to make Italy our permanent full-time home. We're not at the age yet where we get free healthcare services in the United States. And let's be honest, even when they're "free" they're not really free. With our history of medical issues, accidents and previous cancers we just thought it was better to live here full-time and make full use of the medical services Italy has to offer.

The other reason was our large dogs. It's very expensive and very difficult to ship large animals back-and-forth from Italy to United States. So us living part of the year without our dogs and the rest the year with them was just not an option for us.

So think long and hard about how you plan on spending your time in Italy and if you really need an ERV visa. 180 days a year is plenty of time to enjoy the Italian lifestyle if you have a secondary place that you can afford to be in addition to

Italy. It also takes all the tax reporting issues that you will have filing multiple tax returns in at least two countries off the table!

Chapter 2

UNDERSTANDING THE ITALIAN HOME MARKET

OVERVIEW OF ITALIAN REAL ESTATE MARKET TODAY

The Italian real estate market has been a subject of considerable interest, both for domestic investors and international observers. As of today, it stands at a crossroads, shaped by many factors ranging from economic conditions, government policies, and societal trends. Now let's dive into the current state of the Italian residential real estate market, exploring key trends, challenges, and opportunities.

Economic Landscape

The economic condition of a country plays a pivotal role in shaping its real estate market, and Italy is no exception. In recent years, Italy has faced economic challenges, including slowing GDP growth, high public debt, and issues related to labor market efficiency. These factors have contributed to a mixed scenario in the real estate market. Remember that

Italy is not a high income country. The average person in Italy makes less than €33.000/year. A shop clerk or barista might be making only €1200/mo! Therefore property price in Italy are not that high compared to US and other nations. Italy also has an aging population and low birth rate, so there will continue to more and more properties coming on the market if only through attrition.

Another significant aspect was the impact of the COVID-19 pandemic. The real estate sector globally experienced shifts due to the pandemic, and Italy was no different. During the initial stages of the pandemic, the market witnessed a temporary slowdown as uncertainty and lockdown measures affected buyer confidence. However, as the situation stabilized, the real estate market showed signs of resilience.

The residential real estate segment has been a cornerstone of the Italian property market. Despite economic uncertainties, there has been a consistent demand for homes, driven by factors such as population growth, urbanization, and low-interest rates. Cities like Rome, Milan, and Florence continue to attract homebuyers, both domestic and international. That is not to say that all of Italy is a boom area. Southern Italy is still dogged with generations of population flight that affects the Southern Provinces today. Calabria, Campania, and Sicily all have the highest percentage of unemployment in Italy, and also are the epicentre for the abandoned village syndrome that you may have read about. It is these areas where most of the €1 House villages are located. The Italian government has started a new scheme where they only charge a flat 7% tax rate on your pension income if you move to certain southern areas in Italy. But be advised that may still owe income tax on your pension in your home country after you have paid the tax in Italy (if there is any balance left). You will not get double taxed as long as your home country has a tax treaty with Italy which most countries do.

One notable trend is the increased interest in eco-friendly and sustainable housing. As environmental consciousness grows, developers are incorporating green building practices, and buyers are showing a preference for energy-efficient homes. This shift aligns with broader European trends and government initiatives promoting sustainable development.

The rental market, particularly in urban areas, has also seen significant activity. Young professionals and students often prefer renting, contributing to the demand for affordable and well-located rental properties. However, challenges such as housing affordability and limited rental supply persist. Another factor is the increase in tourism which is seeing rentals that would otherwise be used for longterm use, moved into the nightly rental market. Since the increase in tourism is helping increase the GDP for all of Italy. There are no easy answers on how to control the use of rentals.

Market Factors and Pricing

As with any country, Italy's property market is influenced by a many factors ranging from economic conditions and demographic trends to government policies and global events. Understanding the current state of property values requires a comprehensive analysis of these multifaceted dynamics.

Italy, renowned for its rich history, cultural heritage, and scenic landscapes, has always been an attractive destination for property investment. However, the stability of property values in the country is subject to various internal and external factors. You need to look into the economic backdrop, regulatory environment, and societal changes that collectively shape the Italian real estate landscape.

In recent years, Italy has experienced economic challenges that have inevitably impacted its property market. The country has grappled with slow economic growth, high public debt, and political instability. Such macroeconomic factors invariably influence consumer confidence and purchasing power, affecting the demand and supply dynamics in the real estate sector. Despite these challenges, Italy's property market has demonstrated resilience, with certain regions remaining particularly attractive to both domestic and international investors.

The regulatory framework governing the property market in Italy is another crucial aspect influencing stability. Government policies, tax regulations, and legal frameworks play a pivotal role in shaping the real estate landscape. Italy has witnessed changes in property taxation, which can significantly impact property values. Investors keenly monitor these policy developments to anticipate potential shifts in the market. Additionally, legal procedures related to property transactions and ownership rights contribute to the overall perception of stability in the real estate sector.

Societal changes and demographic trends are intrinsic to understanding property value stability. Italy, like many developed nations, is experiencing demographic shifts characterized by an aging population and changing family structures. The demand for different types of properties, such as retirement homes or smaller households, is influenced by these demographic changes. Regions catering to specific demographics may witness variations in property values, and investors must adapt to these evolving trends.

The geographic diversity within Italy also adds complexity to the assessment of property value stability. Different regions exhibit distinct economic activities, cultural attractions, and lifestyle preferences. The real estate markets in big northern cities will have different dynamics compared to rural southern areas or coastal towns. Analyzing regional variations provides a nuanced understanding of the overall stability of property values in Italy.

Impact of Nightly Rental Platforms

In recent years, the rise of the sharing economy has revolutionized the way travellers experience accommodations worldwide. Italy, with its iconic cities, historical landmarks, and diverse landscapes, has not been immune to this shift. The prevalence of Airbnb, Booking, VRBO and the like are leading platforms in the short-term rental market, and have significantly influenced Italy's rental landscape, bringing both opportunities and challenges to the forefront.

The advent of nightly rental platforms in Italy has been met with substantial rental growth, transforming the way tourists seek accommodation. Travellers now have the option to stay in private homes, apartments, or even historic villas, offering a personalized and immersive experience. This surge in popularity has reshaped the dynamics of the traditional rental market.

One of the most significant positive impacts of these rental platforms on Italy's rental market is the economic opportunity it provides for hosts. Homeowners can generate supplemental income by renting out their properties, contributing to their livelihoods and fostering a sense of entrepreneurship within local communities.

Home renting platforms have diversified the range of accommodation options available to travellers. This variety appeals to a broader audience with diverse preferences, from those seeking a quaint countryside retreat to others desiring a modern urban apartment. This diversification has expanded the appeal of Italy as a tourist destination.

However, the rapid growth of these services in Italy has not been without challenges. One notable concern is the impact on the long-term rental market. As property owners pivot towards short-term rentals, the availability of housing for long-term residents diminishes, contributing to housing shortages in some cities. Luckily, Italy is a country blessed with many properties for sale and many opportunities for people to buy and refurbish to either occupy or join the rental business themselves.

The shift towards short-term rentals has sparked concerns about housing shortages, particularly in Italy's urban centers. As properties are converted into vacation rentals, residents, especially in popular tourist destinations, face challenges in finding affordable and suitable long-term housing.

The influx of short-term renters can alter the fabric of local communities. Residential neighborhoods may experience an increase in transient populations, affecting the sense of community cohesion. This shift can be particularly pronounced in historical districts and smaller towns.

In response to the challenges posed by the rise of short-term rentals, Italian authorities and local governments have implemented various regulatory measures. These may include zoning restrictions, occupancy limits, and licensing requirements aimed at balancing the interests of homeowners, tenants, and the broader community.

Policymakers face the challenge of striking a delicate balance between fostering tourism and preserving the availability and affordability of housing for residents. Crafting effective regulations that encourage responsible hosting while mitigating the negative impacts on the rental market remains an ongoing challenge.
Despite the challenges, home rentals has the potential to play a role in promoting sustainable tourism. By connecting travellers directly with local hosts, platforms can contribute to a more authentic and sustainable travel experience, fostering a deeper connection between visitors and the communities they explore.

As Italy grapples with the challenges posed by the sharing economy, finding a harmonious balance between economic opportunities for hosts and the preservation of long-term housing options for residents remains a key task for policymakers. Striking this balance is essential to ensure that the allure of Italy as a tourist destination does not come at the expense of its residents' access to affordable and suitable housing.

Chapter 3

LEGAL & REGULATORY LANDSCAPE

THE ITALIAN LEGAL SYSTEM AS IT RELATES TO PROPERTIES

Overview of the legal system in Italy

There's simply not a way to make a chapter of a book all about the Italian legal system a fun and mesmerizing thing to read... Even for Italians, the legal system in Italy is confusing. Normally a simple purchase of a house shouldn't require you to get a lawyer in Italy as the notary will be responsible for making sure that your purchase is clean with no future problems able to come and bite you but it still pays to read this chapter to try to get an understanding of the various laws and their meaning in Italy.

One of the fundamental principles of the Italian legal system is the recognition and protection of property rights. The Italian Constitution, adopted in 1948, enshrines the right to property in its Article 42. This constitutional protection serves as a cornerstone for the legal regime surrounding properties in Italy. It establishes the importance of balancing individual property rights with the common good, emphasizing the role of the state in regulating property relations.

Property transactions in Italy are subject to meticulous legal procedures. The transfer of real estate typically involves a public notary who plays a crucial role in ensuring the legality and validity of the transaction. The notary is responsible for drafting the deed of sale, verifying the seller's title, and registering the transaction with the land registry. The Italian Land Registry (Catasto) is a central institution that maintains public records of properties, providing transparency and legal certainty.

The process of property registration is a key element in the Italian legal system. It not only ensures the clarity of property ownership but also acts as a safeguard against fraudulent transactions. The land registry contains essential information, including property boundaries, ownership details, and any encumbrances or mortgages. Property buyers, as a standard practice, conduct due diligence to verify the accuracy of these records before completing a transaction.

Land use and zoning regulations are integral components of the legal framework governing properties in Italy. Local municipalities have the authority to establish zoning plans, specifying the permitted uses for different areas. These regulations aim to manage urban development, preserve cultural heritage, and balance environmental concerns. Property owners must adhere to these regulations, and any deviations may lead to legal consequences.

Leases and rental agreements are subject to specific legal provisions in Italy. The Italian Civil Code governs landlord-tenant relationships, defining the rights and obligations of both parties. Lease agreements typically include details such as the duration of the lease, rent amounts, and maintenance responsibilities. The legal framework provides tenants with protection against arbitrary eviction and ensures a fair balance between the interests of landlords and tenants.

Property taxation in Italy is another significant aspect of the legal system. Taxes on real estate include the Imposta Municipale Unica (IMU), a municipal property tax, and the Imposta sul Reddito delle Persone Fisiche (IRPEF), an income tax that also applies to rental income. Additionally, there may be regional and local taxes, adding complexity to the overall taxation structure. Property owners must comply with these tax obligations to avoid legal consequences.

In the event of property disputes, the legal system in Italy provides avenues for resolution. Civil litigation is the primary mechanism for resolving conflicts related to properties. The judicial system is structured hierarchically, with various levels of courts, including the Court of Cassation as the highest court of appeal. Alternative dispute resolution methods, such as mediation and arbitration, also play a role in resolving property disputes, offering a faster and less formal option.

The preservation of cultural heritage is a distinctive feature of the Italian legal system. The country's rich historical and artistic legacy has led to stringent regulations to protect cultural properties. The Code of Cultural Heritage and Landscape sets forth measures to safeguard Italy's cultural heritage, imposing restrictions on alterations or demolitions of protected properties.

The legal system in Italy relating to properties is a complex and multifaceted framework that reflects the country's legal traditions, constitutional principles, and societal values. From property transactions and registration to landlord-tenant relationships and dispute resolution, the legal landscape ensures the protection of property rights while considering broader societal interests.

Key Legal Requirements for Expats

Italy attracts a significant number of foreign investors interested in the real estate market. While Italy generally welcomes foreign investment, there are key regulations and considerations that foreigners must be aware of when engaging in real estate transactions within the country.

One of the primary regulations that foreigners encounter is the reciprocity principle. Italy often applies this principle, meaning that the treatment of foreign investors in Italy is contingent upon the treatment that Italian citizens receive in the foreign investor's home country. If a foreigner's home country grants Italian citizens the right to own property, Italy typically reciprocates. However, the specifics of reciprocity can vary, and it is essential for foreign investors to verify the current status of reciprocity agreements between their home country and Italy.

Foreigners looking to purchase property in Italy should also be aware of the legal requirements related to obtaining a codice fiscale. The codice fiscale is a unique identification code, similar to a tax identification number (like a social security number in the United States), and is necessary for various transactions in Italy, including real estate purchases. Foreigners can obtain a codice fiscale through the Italian consulate or local tax office. Your real estate agent may be able to help you secure your codice fiscale

In some cases, non-EU foreigners may need to obtain prior approval from the Italian Ministry of Defense to acquire property in certain strategic or border areas. This is part of

Italy's effort to safeguard national security interests and prevent unauthorized acquisitions in sensitive regions.

Another crucial consideration for foreign investors is Italy's strict anti-money laundering regulations. The Italian legal framework has implemented European Union directives to combat money laundering and terrorist financing. As a result, both Italian and foreign buyers are subject to due diligence procedures, and real estate professionals are required to verify the identity of their clients.

The Italian legal system also provides mechanisms to facilitate real estate transactions for foreigners. A power of attorney is commonly used to authorize a representative to act on behalf of the buyer or seller, allowing flexibility in completing transactions, especially for those who may not be physically present in Italy during the entire process.

In the rental market, foreigners entering into lease agreements should be familiar with the regulations outlined in the Italian Civil Code. The rights and obligations of landlords and tenants are clearly defined, ensuring a fair and transparent rental relationship. Lease agreements should be carefully reviewed, and any specific provisions or requirements should be clearly understood by both parties.

Lastly, cultural heritage protection regulations can impact real estate transactions involving historic properties. Foreigners interested in purchasing or renovating properties with historical significance must comply with strict regulations to preserve Italy's cultural heritage. Approvals from relevant authorities may be required for alterations or renovations to protect the integrity of historically significant structures.

While Italy is generally open to foreign investment in its real estate market, understanding the key regulations and legal considerations is essential for a smooth and compliant transaction. From reciprocity principles to taxation, anti-money laundering measures, and cultural heritage protection, foreign investors must navigate these aspects to ensure a successful and legally sound real estate venture in Italy.

Legal Process for Property Transactions

Purchasing real estate in Italy as a foreigner involves navigating a detailed legal process that may differ from the procedures in your home country. The Italian real estate market is renowned for its cultural and bureaucratic nuances, and understanding the legal framework is crucial to a successful transaction. In this section, we will explore the various steps and considerations involved in the process of foreigners acquiring real estate in Italy.

1. Preliminary Research and Due Diligence

Before getting into the legal intricacies, it is essential to conduct thorough research. This involves identifying the location, type of property, and budget constraints. You should familiarize yourself with the Italian property market, property values, and potential risks. Engaging a local real estate agent can provide valuable insights and assistance in this initial phase. With the large number or real estate listing sites on the internet, you should be able to begin your search easily from the comfort of your own home.

Once you have established an area that you think will be the right one for your new home or investment purchase, that is the time to reach out to a local agent to get serious on seeing properties in person. Remember that the system of selling houses in Italy will probably be unique from where you live now. There are very few houses that are sold on an exclusive basis with a realtor, so many realtors will claim to be the "listing agent". They may even be in competition with the owner of the house themselves because the owner will not pay an agent for selling their home if they didn't bring the buyer themselves. You will find the same home listed many times on the same website because agents in Italy are well known for "pirating" listings or just taking photos of homes that are for sale and making their own listing for that home, in hopes of finding new clients or of finding an actual buyer to present to the owner of the home.

2. Codice Fiscale (Tax Payer Number)

One of the first steps for a foreigner interested in purchasing real estate in Italy is obtaining a Codice Fiscale, which is an Italian Taxpayer Number, similar to a United States Social Security number. This unique identification number is required for various transactions, including property purchases. Foreigners can acquire a Codice Fiscale from the Agenzia delle Entrate (Revenue Agency) by submitting the necessary documentation including a valid passport. It may be possible for your real estate agent to apply for and secure the Codice Fiscale for you in your absence. You will need an Italian bank account as well to facilitate the transfer of money and payment of the various taxes, agents, fees, etc. involved in buying a home. The Codice Fiscale is required to open a bank account as well.

3. Compromesso (Preliminary Contract)

In Italy, the "Compromesso" is a preliminary contract in real estate transactions, serving as a legally binding agreement between the buyer and seller before the final deed of sale. Also known as the "Preliminary Contract," it outlines the terms and conditions of the property transfer. The Compromesso typically includes details such as the property description, purchase price, payment terms, and the expected date of the final deed.

Upon signing the Compromesso, the buyer usually pays a deposit, ranging from 10% to 30% of the property's value. This deposit is a key aspect of the agreement and serves as a guarantee of commitment from both parties. If the buyer decides not to proceed with the purchase without valid reasons, they risk forfeiting the deposit. Conversely, if the seller backs out without just cause, they may be required to refund double the deposit to the buyer.

The Compromesso is a crucial step in the Italian property buying process, providing a level of security and clarity for both parties while finalizing the details before the official transfer of ownership through the notarial deed.

4. Due Diligence by the Notary

In Italy, a notary plays a pivotal role in ensuring the validity and safety of a real estate transaction for the buyer. The notary is a quasi-public officer appointed by the state, and their primary responsibility is to oversee and authenticate legal documents, including property transactions.

Firstly, the notary conducts thorough due diligence on the property, verifying its legal status, ownership history, and any encumbrances. They ensure that the property has a clear title, free from disputes or legal issues that could affect the sale. This comprehensive examination helps prevent any surprises or legal complications for the buyer in the future.

During the transaction, the notary drafts and reviews the preliminary contract, such as the Compromesso, ensuring that all terms and conditions are fair, legal, and protective of both parties' interests. They also verify the legitimacy of the parties involved, confirming the seller's ownership rights and the buyer's financial capacity.

The notary is responsible for collecting and disbursing funds related to the transaction. They often hold the buyer's deposit in a secure escrow account until the final deed is executed, providing financial security for both parties. Additionally, the notary calculates and oversees the payment of taxes and fees associated with the sale, ensuring compliance with legal requirements.

On the completion day, the notary presides over the signing of the final deed of sale, known as the "atto notarile." They authenticate the document, confirming the transfer of ownership and updating the property registry accordingly. The notary also ensures that all outstanding obligations, such as outstanding utility bills and property taxes, are settled before the transfer is completed.

Ultimately, the notary's role is integral to safeguarding the buyer's interests by guaranteeing the legality, transparency, and fairness of the real estate transaction in Italy. Buyers can rely on the notary to provide expert guidance, mitigate risks, and ensure that the property purchase is a secure and valid investment.5. Property Valuation and Survey

It is common for buyers to engage a surveyor to assess the property's condition and value. While this step is not legally mandatory, it provides the buyer with an independent evaluation and helps in negotiating the final purchase price.

5. Signing the Final Deed (Rogito)

Signing the final deed, known as "Rogito," is a crucial step in completing a real estate transaction in Italy. The process involves several key steps:

A. Notary Presence: The signing of the Rogito takes place in the presence of a notary, a public officer appointed by the state. The notary ensures the legality and validity of the transaction.

B. Verification of Identity: The notary verifies the identities of both the buyer and seller to confirm their legal capacity to engage in the transaction.

C. Payment Confirmation: The notary verifies that the buyer has paid the full purchase price and any associated costs. This may include taxes, fees, and the remaining balance after the initial deposit.

D. Reading of the Deed: The notary reads the entire deed aloud to both parties, ensuring that they understand and agree to the terms outlined in the document. Any questions or concerns can be addressed at this stage. This can take hours.

E. Signatures: Once satisfied with the terms, both the buyer and seller sign the Rogito in the presence of the notary. The notary then signs and affixes their official seal to the document.

F. Handover of Keys: Following the signing, the seller typically hands over the keys and possession of the property to the buyer. This signifies the completion of the transfer of ownership.

G. Registration: The notary is responsible for registering the Rogito with the local land registry office, updating the property records to reflect the new owner.

The Rogito is a legally binding document, and its signing marks the official conclusion of the real estate transaction. It provides clarity and security for both parties, confirming the transfer of ownership in a transparent and enforceable manner. The notary's role in this process is crucial to ensuring the legality and validity of the transaction, offering protection to both the buyer and seller.

6. Registration of the Deed

Following the signing of the rogito, the notary registers the deed with the local land registry office. This step is crucial for validating the property transfer and updating the public records. The registration process involves paying the necessary fees and taxes.

7. Tax Considerations

Buyers must be aware of the various taxes associated with property transactions in Italy. The main taxes include the Imposta di Registro (registration tax), Imposta Catastale (cadastral tax), and Imposta Ipotecaria (mortgage tax). These taxes are typically borne by the buyer and can vary based on factors such as property type and location. Taxes will be covered in detail in Chapter 8

8. Currency Exchange and Banking

As a foreign buyer, it is essential to consider the currency exchange process. Transactions are mostly conducted in euros, so understanding the exchange rates and choosing a reputable bank or currency exchange service is crucial to avoid unnecessary costs. It is important to watch the exchange rates because they fluctuate and even a small percentage change in the rate can have an outsized impact on your purchase because of the large amount of money that can be involved in a purchase.

9. Legal Representation

While legal representation is not mandatory in Italy, many foreigners choose to engage a lawyer to navigate the legal complexities on their behalf. A qualified lawyer can provide valuable advice, review contracts, and ensure that the buyer's interests are protected throughout the process.

10. Residency and Visa Considerations

Purchasing real estate in Italy may have implications for residency and visa requirements. Normally to get a Elective Residency Visa, you must show the consulate that you have a home in Italy, or a minimum 12 month lease in force. Understanding the potential implications and consulting with immigration authorities is advisable in such cases.

11. Financing and Mortgages

If financing is required, buyers should explore mortgage options available in Italy. Local banks and financial institutions may have specific requirements for foreign applicants, so it is crucial to understand the terms, interest rates, and repayment conditions associated with mortgage agreements.

12. Community Rules and Condominiums

In Italy, many properties, especially in urban areas, are part of condominiums governed by specific rules and regulations. Buyers need to be aware of these rules, including any associated fees and obligations, as they can impact the overall cost of property ownership.

13. Estate Agents and Negotiations

Working with a reputable estate agent can simplify the buying process. Agents assist in property searches, negotiations, and liaising with the seller. In Italy, the buyer pays the buyers agent, normally a 3% commission on the purchase price of the property. In the event that the property has a very low purchase price, the agent will want to negotiate a flat fee for their services. Selling properties in Italy is a very complicated task and good agents are worth their weight in gold. They will be helping you both during and after the sale.

14. Inheritance Laws

Italy has specific inheritance laws that may affect the passing on of property to heirs. Understanding these laws and considering the implications for future generations is important for long-term property ownership planning.

The legal process for foreigners purchasing real estate in Italy is a multifaceted journey that requires careful consideration of cultural, legal, and financial aspects. Engaging local professionals, such as notaries and lawyers, is highly recommended to navigate the complexities and ensure a smooth and legally sound property acquisition. By understanding the nuances of the Italian real estate market and adhering to the prescribed legal procedures, foreigners can embark on a successful journey to own a piece of Italy's rich and diverse landscape.

Chapter 4

FINANCING YOUR HOME PURCHASE

UNDERSTANDING ITALIAN MORTGAGES AND FINANCING

Financing Options for Expats

Financing real estate purchases in Italy as a foreigner is a complex landscape of financial options. Italy has drawn many international buyers seeking to invest in its real estate market. Understanding the various financing avenues is crucial for foreigners looking to make this investment. Several options exist, ranging from traditional mortgages to alternative financing methods.

One of the primary avenues for financing real estate in Italy is through traditional mortgages offered by Italian banks. Foreigners can approach these banks to secure a mortgage, but the process can be intricate. Italian banks typically require a substantial down payment, often ranging from 20% to 50% of the property's value. Additionally, applicants must meet stringent credit criteria, and documentation requirements may be extensive. It is advisable for potential buyers to engage the services of a local financial advisor to navigate through the intricacies of the mortgage application process.

In recent years, some Italian banks have introduced specific mortgage products designed for foreign investors. These products may offer more flexible terms and conditions, catering to the unique needs of international buyers. However, interest rates and fees associated with these mortgages may be higher compared to those available to Italian citizens.

Another option for financing real estate in Italy is seeking assistance from international banks that operate in the country. Many global financial institutions have branches in major Italian cities, and some specialize in providing mortgages to non-resident foreigners. These banks may have a better understanding of the specific needs and challenges faced by international buyers, offering tailored financial solutions. However, applicants should be prepared for a thorough evaluation process and potentially higher interest rates.

Private lenders and mortgage brokers also play a role in financing real estate purchases in Italy. These entities can provide a range of financing options, and their flexibility may be appealing to foreigners facing challenges with traditional lenders. However, it's essential to exercise caution when dealing with private lenders, as terms and conditions can vary widely, and some may carry higher risks.

In recent years, Italy has seen the emergence of crowdfunding platforms focused on real estate. These platforms allow multiple investors, including foreigners, to pool funds for property acquisitions. While this method provides a unique way to finance real estate, potential investors must carefully evaluate the risks and returns associated with crowdfunding, as the real estate market can be subject to fluctuations.

Some foreigners choose to finance their real estate purchases in Italy through seller financing arrangements. In this scenario, the buyer negotiates financing directly with the seller, bypassing traditional lending institutions. While this approach may offer more flexibility in terms of down payments and interest rates, it requires a level of trust between the buyer and seller, and legal advice is crucial to ensure the transaction's legitimacy.

Leasing with an option to buy is another alternative for foreigners seeking to invest in Italian real estate. This arrangement allows the buyer to lease the property with an option to purchase it at a later date. While this method doesn't provide immediate ownership, it can be a strategic way for foreigners to assess the property and the market before committing to a purchase.

Financing real estate purchases in Italy as a foreigner involves navigating a diverse array of options. From traditional mortgages offered by Italian banks to international lenders, private financing, crowdfunding, seller financing, and leasing with an option to buy, each option has its unique advantages and challenges. Prospective buyers should carefully evaluate their financial situation, seek professional advice, and choose the financing method that aligns with their goals and risk tolerance. Engaging with local experts, including real estate agents, lawyers, and financial advisors, can be instrumental in ensuring a smooth and successful real estate investment in Italy.

Overview of Getting a Mortgage for Real Property in Italy:

1. **Research and Planning:** Begin by identifying the property you want to purchase. Research various locations, property types, and prices to find a suitable option.

2. **Budget Assessment:** Determine your budget and assess your financial capability to determine the mortgage amount you may need.

3. **Preliminary Agreement (Compromesso):** Once you find a property, a preliminary agreement, known as "Compromesso," is typically signed between the buyer and seller. This document outlines the terms and conditions of the sale. Your deposit, usually around 10% of the property's value, is paid upon signing the Compromesso.

4. **Due Diligence:** Conduct thorough due diligence on the property. Verify legal ownership, check for any liens or encumbrances, and ensure that the property complies with zoning regulations. Engage professionals, such as a notary, to assist with the due diligence process.

5. **Mortgage Pre-Approval:** Before proceeding, it's advisable to obtain mortgage pre-approval from a bank. This involves submitting your financial documents to demonstrate your creditworthiness. The bank assesses your income, credit history, and other financial details to determine the maximum mortgage amount you qualify for. You will probably find that if you are not a current resident in Italy

(that is a foreign citizen living full time in Italy with an official long term visa), that you will have a difficult time securing a mortgage for a property purchase in Italy, regardless of the strength of your financials. You may be better off securing financing in your home country through a broker or bank. Many people may also be able to finance the new home purchase using a HELOC or LOC tied to real property you own in your country of origin.

6. Finalizing the Mortgage Application: Once you decide on a specific property, you can finalize your mortgage application with the chosen bank.

Submit all required documents, which may include proof of income, employment history, identification, and details about the property.

7. Property Valuation: The bank typically conducts a property valuation to determine its market value. This step is crucial for the bank to assess the property's worth in relation to the loan amount. The loan can be based on this amount of appraised value. Therefore, if there is a short fall in appraised value, the bank may ask for an increased downpayment from the buyer. If there is a higher appraised value than the asking price, the bank may loan on that amount as well, effectively lowering the amount of downpayment needed from the buyer. Each bank has their own guidelines so check with them on exact policies.

8. Mortgage Offer: If the property valuation is satisfactory, the bank issues a mortgage offer. This document details the loan terms, interest rates, and repayment conditions. Review the offer carefully and seek legal advice if necessary. You may find that different banks have different terms and it pays to shop around. The biggest differences will probably be in the deposit required, and length or repayment terms.

9. Notary Public Involvement: In Italy, property transactions require the involvement of a notary public. The notary ensures the legality of the transaction, conducts the necessary checks, and drafts the official deed of sale. Notaries in Italy are quasi-official agents of the government. They just don't tell you where to sign. They have a fiduciary duty to ensure that all the aspects of the property are in order and they guarantee the "Free and Clear" aspect of the purchase, so that there are no surprises after the closing of the sale.

10. Closing and Signing the Mortgage Deed: The final step involves signing the mortgage deed at the notary's office. This document outlines the terms and conditions of the mortgage, and both parties sign it in the presence of the notary. Remember that it is quite common for there to be a "Power of Attorney" in effect for your property purchase, especially if either the buyer or seller is a foreign resident. If you need a "POA" try to find someone that is fluent in Italian and English, because that will save you the translation fee. In Italy, all documents at closing are read out loud by the notary, verbatim! This is a time consuming prospect… A translator for your closing can easily be €800, so it may even be cheaper to just have a POA go for the signing and forgo the translation fee.

Simultaneously, the main deed of sale is signed, transferring ownership of the property to the buyer. All the points above are in force for this part of the signing too. A typical signing can take 2-4 hours depending on the complexity of the deed and purchase.

11. Mortgage Registration: The mortgage deed is then registered at the land registry to secure the bank's interest in the property. This registration is crucial for legal recognition of the mortgage.

12. Repayment and Ongoing Obligations: After obtaining the mortgage, you'll start repaying the loan according to the agreed-upon schedule. Ensure timely payments to avoid any penalties.

Additionally, property owners in Italy are subject to property taxes and other ongoing obligations, which should be understood and managed.

Getting a mortgage for real property in Italy involves a series of well-defined steps, from preliminary agreements to finalizing the mortgage at the notary's office. Thorough research, financial planning, and legal assistance are crucial throughout the process to ensure a smooth and successful property purchase. Remember to work closely with professionals, including real estate agents, notaries, and financial advisors, to navigate the complexities of the Italian real estate market and mortgage system.

Chapter 5

TYPES OF HOMES TO BUY

VILLAS, HISTORIC CENTERS AND MODERN HOMES

Italy boasts a rich and diverse housing landscape that reflects its historical, cultural, and architectural heritage. The country's housing options can be broadly categorized into three main types: Villas, Historic Center Homes, and Modern Homes. Each type has its unique characteristics, reflecting different periods of Italian history and cultural influences.

Italian Villa

Villas & Single Family Homes

Villas are an iconic and quintessential representation of Italian luxury and elegance. These grand residences typically feature expansive grounds, lush gardens, and are often situated in the countryside or on the outskirts of cities. Villas have a long history in Italy, dating back to ancient Roman times when they were initially rural farmhouses. Over the centuries, they evolved into opulent estates that served as summer retreats for the wealthy.

Characteristics of Villas & SFH's

Architectural Style: Villas in Italy display a variety of architectural styles, ranging from Renaissance and Baroque to Neoclassical and modern designs. The architectural features often include stately facades, symmetrical layouts, and grand entrances.

Expansive Grounds: One of the distinguishing features of villas is their extensive grounds. These may include manicured gardens, orchards, vineyards, and sometimes even private lakes. The outdoor spaces are designed to complement the grandeur of the main residence.

Historical Significance: Some villas in Italy have historical significance, having been owned by noble families or historical figures. These properties may feature frescoes, intricate stucco work, and other period details that highlight their cultural and artistic importance.

Modern Amenities: While preserving their historical charm, many villas have been renovated to incorporate modern

Homes in Montepulciano, Tuscany

amenities such as swimming pools, state-of-the-art kitchens, and updated infrastructure.

Location: Villas are commonly found in the countryside, providing a peaceful and scenic retreat. However, some urban areas may also have villas, especially in the suburbs.

Historic Center Homes

Italy's historic city centers are renowned for their narrow cobblestone streets, medieval architecture, and vibrant atmosphere. Historic center homes, often apartments or townhouses, are an integral part of the urban housing fabric. These residences offer a unique living experience, blending the charm of historical architecture with the convenience of city living.

Characteristics of Historic Center Homes

Architectural Diversity: The historic center homes in Italy showcase a diverse range of architectural styles, reflecting the evolution of the cities over the centuries. From medieval structures with wooden beams to elegant Renaissance townhouses, each property tells a story of the city's past.

Compact Living: Due to the limited space within city centers, historic homes are often characterized by a compact layout. High ceilings, small balconies, and clever use of space are common features.

Cultural Heritage: Living in a historic center home allows residents to be immersed in the cultural heritage of the city. Museums, theaters, and historical landmarks are often within walking distance, contributing to a vibrant and dynamic lifestyle.

Renovation Challenges: Many historic center homes require careful renovation to modernize living spaces while preserving the original character. Renovations must adhere to strict regulations aimed at protecting the cultural and architectural integrity of the area.

Proximity to Amenities: One of the advantages of historic center living is the proximity to amenities such as shops, restaurants, and public transportation. Residents can enjoy the convenience of urban life while surrounded by historical landmarks.

Modern Home with Old World Touches

Characteristics of Modern Homes

Contemporary Design: Modern homes in Italy often feature sleek lines, large windows, and open Italy has embraced modern architecture, and contemporary homes can be found in both urban and suburban settings. Modern homes in Italy showcase cutting-edge design, sustainable features, and a departure from traditional architectural styles. These residences cater to open floor plans. Architects incorporate innovative materials and design principles to create homes that are both functional and aesthetically pleasing.

Energy Efficiency: Many modern homes prioritize sustainability and energy efficiency. This includes features such as solar panels, efficient insulation, and smart home technologies to reduce environmental impact and energy consumption.

Urban and Suburban Settings: Modern homes can be found in urban areas, where architects transform old industrial spaces into stylish lofts, as well as in suburban settings where spacious, contemporary villas offer a comfortable and luxurious lifestyle.

Integration of Nature: Some modern homes in Italy seamlessly integrate with the natural surroundings, featuring expansive windows that provide panoramic views of the countryside or coastal landscapes. Outdoor living spaces, such as terraces and gardens, are often designed to enhance the connection with nature.

Innovative Materials: Architects often experiment with innovative materials in the construction of modern homes, including glass, steel, and eco-friendly building materials. These choices contribute to the overall aesthetic and functionality of the properties.

Italy's diverse housing landscape offers a range of options catering to various preferences and lifestyles. Villas represent the epitome of luxury and historical opulence, while historic center homes allow residents to immerse themselves in the rich cultural tapestry of Italy's urban centers. On the other hand, modern homes showcase the country's embrace of contemporary design and sustainability.

Whether you seek the tranquility of the countryside, the cultural richness of historic city living, or the modern comforts of cutting-edge architecture, Italy's housing options provide a captivating blend of tradition and innovation.

€1 Homes Explained

The idea of buying a home for just one euro is alluring to millions of people. In the last 10 years, many dozens of Italian municipalities have begun offering abandon homes for the nominal fee of €1. This resulted in a media frenzy and also dreams among many people of being able to move to Italy and secure housing for just one euro. Like every dream, this one often resulted in a huge clash with reality. Many of the homes did not sell for the touted €1, but we're put into a bidding process and sold for thousands of euros more.

Most of the homes that are sold this way need extensive remodeling and not just simple painting and a refresh. It's imperative if you're thinking about buying a home in this fashion that you visit the area where you're looking before you make any offer. It may sound counterintuitive to spend a few thousand dollars traveling to the place where you want to buy a €1 home, but remember that you're going to be tied to this property for many years, and you will be putting tens of thousands of euros into it to make it habitable. That type of investment requires a lot of due diligence. We should mention here that the cost of doing remodeling in Italy is in line with other European nations. If a home has been sitting for 50 years unused, you can be guaranteed that all the piping and all the electrical will have to be changed. The cost of completely redoing the waste water in a home could be well over €10,000. Having to completely redo the electrical system could set you back another €10,000 or more depending on the size of the house.

The stark reality is that these homes are usually in places where there is such a huge decline in population that it becomes impossible to sell the homes at any price. Almost without fail, you can find houses that are in habitable condition in the same areas for less than the cost of remodeling a €1 home. So the question becomes are you buying a home in that area because you want to live in that area, or is it because you think you're going to find free housing? If it's the latter, you had better do excellent due diligence to make sure you're not buying into a false dream.

It is also important to check the general infrastructure of the area you were looking at for when you are buying a €1 home. Many of these towns and villages have small populations and may be some distance from the next major city. Especially for people of a certain age like retirees, it is so important to have good quality medical care at your fingertips, that buying a house in a remote part of the country could be life-threatening. Colossal need to check for the availability of simple things like large high-quality supermarkets to give you the selection that you are more than likely comfortable with choosing from, especially for fresh meats, fruits and vegetables.

It is admirable that these towns want to turn themselves around and become areas of easy and fruitful living again. But the harsh reality is that without significant infrastructure investment at the corporate, small business and governmental level, these towns will never be able to find their footing again.

Chapter 6

WORKING WITH ITALIAN REAL ESTATE AGENTS

IMPORTANT CONSIDERATIONS FOR CHOOSING AGENTS

Working with real estate agents in Italy is vastly different than what I had experienced working for 25 years in commercial and residential real estate in the United States. Gone are Sunday morning texts to an agent to go view a house that had just came on the market (nobody works on Sunday!). Gone are quickly answered questions about taxes, or schools, or comps (comparisons) in the area because there is no multiple listing service system in Italy with the answers. It is virtually impossible to get "sold" prices on properties to get a feel for what things are really selling for. It takes an amateur sleuth to even be able to figure out how many days a certain property has been on the market (DOM). That DOM metric was one of my best tools for figuring out what sort of offer to make on a particular property.

Real estate agents play a important role in facilitating property transactions, serving as intermediaries between buyers and sellers. In Italy, licensed real estate agents, or "agenzie immobiliari," are regulated by specific laws to ensure professionalism, transparency, and ethical conduct in the industry. But like elsewhere in the world, that doesn't mean that they are all winners… some agents are lazy, others are only going to steer you towards properties where they are going to make the best commissions. The worst sin of all in real estate is for 'buyers agents" to not get you the lowest price possible because it helps inflate their earning from the sale.

I was lucky that I was born very extroverted. Even in a new environment I meet people quickly and regardless of language barriers, I quickly form a network of people that I can use to find other people who can help me towards my goals. Italy is truly the land of "I know a guy who knows a guy…!" Once you are in an area where you are likely to want to get serious about finding a home to buy, whether personal or investment, you should start to put out feelers for the people working in real estate.

You are going to be spending your hard earned money to buy something in Italy, and regardless of the property price you can demand very good service from your agent. Don't ever feel that you have to settle for subpar service here just because you aren't Italian. This property purchase you are thinking about might be a large percentage of all the money that you have worked your whole life for. Make sure you don't settle for less because you are an outsider.

Benefits of Working with Real Estate Agents

Local Expertise
Real estate agents *should* possess in-depth knowledge of their respective regions, providing clients with valuable insights into local markets, neighborhoods, and property values. This local expertise is especially crucial for

international buyers unfamiliar with the nuances of the Italian real estate landscape. I personally feel that you should come and spend many weeks if not months staying in the place you are thinking about buying a property in. If you can't get away to see the property and spend a few weeks exploring the area, is it really the time for you to be going through the trouble and expense of buying it in the first place?

I hear so many stories from my subscribers of my YouTube channel about people who were sorry that they had made an offer on a property that they had never even seen in person. It is impossible to tell the exact condition from only a video or photos. Believe me when I tell you that it is easy to make a property look nice on video even though it isn't that great. I walk some really distressed properties every month for BradsWorld filming and I can honestly say that I am surprised sometimes how nice they come across on the video versus the reality of what I experienced in the tour. You can't smell the lovely Renaissance sewer smell, or you don't see the mold in the corner, and of course it's always hard to see rodent feces and other unpleasantries.

Navigating Legalities
Like everywhere in the world, Italian real estate transactions involve complex legal procedures and paperwork. A good agent should be able to help you through most of this.... But an excellent agent will know when to bring in the other professionals that might make up your team like lawyers or accountants. The notary in Italy is really the most important person in the process as far as legal questions go. They are a quasi-agent of the government itself and will be ensuring that the property once closed is your forever and free from any encumbrances. They are such sticklers that I even had to change my legal signature here in Italy to sign all the documents. My original signature looked something like a

really bad EKG.... Just a scribble and done. It was easy to sign 100 times in 5 mins. It Italy I needed to sign out my full name, including my middle name and it had to be legible.

Property Selection
Before you engage an agent in a particular area, you should be very familiar with that market. It is so easy today with online listings to have a good understanding of the market. Your first conversation with an agent should not be so general that they don't know if you are looking for something 50 MQ or 300 MQ. (If you don't know what MQ is yet, you really need to start researching the terms here in real estate listings in Italy!). Everything is done in metric, so MQ is Square Meters (Metri Quadrati). Your agent needs to be able to narrow down the search a lot so the more information you have to give them the better. And be very honest about your budget. Remember also that you will probably not be able to get a loan from an Italian bank unless you are a resident or citizen of Italy.

Negotiation Skills
You are really going to have to be familiar with the local market to be able to help your real estate agent negotiate. I had a situation where I was looking at a property in Lucca, Italy in 2021. It was a very nicely done three story building that had an en-suite with a king size bed, living room and large full bath on each of the three floors. It was already done with all the things you need for a successful rental unit for nightly rentals like entry keypads for each unique apartment. But I felt the asking price off €400.000 was a bit steep. Remember this was still the time when we were coming out of Covid... I told my agent team that I had been assigned from the agency that was listing it that I was only comfortable offering €310.000. It was a tough offer but I think it was workable. The agent I had said he would not submit that offer as it would offend the seller... Needless to

say I found another agent and passed on that property. Full disclosure, I probably should have paid a little more for it than €310K and closed the deal. Lucca has absolutely exploded over the last few years and prices are up 30-40%.

All of this is to say that you need to be comfortable with what you are offering, and even more importantly you need to know how the market pricing is to make sure that you get the very best pricing you can, without passing up on something that was actually a good deal.

Language and Cultural Bridge
I am a real stickler on one point in both my dealings personally and also the agents that I work with on my YouTube channel BradsWorld. You need to work with an agent that is conversationally proficient in your language if you're not comfortable speaking in Italian. These transactions are too important to you to rely on third-party sings things incorrectly or trying to use apps like Google translate. Your agent should be able to carry on a comfortable conversation in your language. I have an agent that speaks for different languages besides Italian fluently. It's not impossible to find someone like that, but you may need to search diligently.

Challenges and Considerations

Agent Selection
While Italy has many reputable real estate agents, choosing the right one requires careful consideration. Prospective clients should research an agent's reputation, experience, and client testimonials to ensure a reliable partnership. You should ask around in the town or city where you are looking to find suitable agents and then meet with each one to find the best match for your personality. If you are trying to find an agent and you are outside of Italy, you are going to be at

a disadvantage. But it is not impossible to do. I recommend NOT using the agent that is assigned to you or trying to sell the property that you saw online that you are interested in. Remember that in Italy there are very few exclusive listings. Many agents here copy other agents listings and you may see the same home listed up to 10 times. I prefer to use agents that have a lot of properties that may not be shown online (pocket listings) and those properties will not have been picked over. Also, agents that are life long residents will know everybody at least in smaller towns, and will know which properties are available to purchase even if it is just a whisper in their ear.

Cultural Differences
Italy runs at it's own pace…. It can be frustrating to a buyer from out of the country. I know for me it was a very difficult change to make and I am still not 100% comfortable with how things are done here. I wonder "why there can not be lockboxes on properties here?". Every time you want to see a property, the owner must be found. Then the keys need to be procured from them or their family or agents. Maybe the agency that might have the keys doesn't want you agent to show the property to you because then they are only going to get the sellers fee, not the buyers fee too. I have had this happen more than once. They flatly refuse to work with another agency.

Another issue that comes up is the timing of things. I am used to making an offer and having it rejected or accepted in a day or two at most. Here in Italy it might take a week to get the offer presented to the owners. I had a recent experience where the offer wasn't presented to the owners until all the papers on the house had been procured from the small town where the house was located…. Why should I wait to have the documents in hand for the house to make an offer, when I am more interested in whether they would accept my offer that was 10% below asking, then they can round up the documents? One had nothing to do with the other. In the end it worked out and offer accepted, but it took more than a week!

Fees and Commissions
Real estate agents in Italy typically charge a commission fee upon successful completion of a transaction. It is essential for clients to clarify the fee structure with their chosen agent upfront to avoid any misunderstandings later in the process. The fee for the buyers agent is borne by the buyer. Normally in Italy it is a 3% fee, but in the case of very low priced real estate, there may be a flat fee charged of €3.000-4.500. Normally this flat fee is charged on properties selling for less than €100.000.

Make sure you pick an agent that you are very comfortable working with. There should never be a feeling like you don't want to bug them. An agent that can sell a very nice property in Italy may make more on that one transaction than many people make with a good job salary here in a year. Remember that the average salary for an office worker in Italy is around €30.000/year, or roughly the commission on a sale of a house at €1.000.000. They should work diligently to help you close your sale.

I would also like to add here that there is something here called, "Real Estate Tourists". Many people find it fun to shop around for real estate when they don't have a serious expectation to close a sale. As agents work on commission this is a total waste of their limited resources. If you are thinking of buying something in the next "few years", you will probably not get a serious agent to do much leg work for you... And why should they, whatever is on the market now that is decent will not be on the market in a few years. You can get a good idea of pricing and quality from looking at listings, it isn't necessary to go out and spend days looking at properties in person. Keep that in mind and present you situation honestly so you can help the agents best use their resources. You will appreciate it when the time comes that you are really serious about getting a deal done!

Chapter 7

PROPERTY AND OTHER TAX IMPLICATIONS

HOW TAXES WILL AFFECT YOU IN ITALY

The Tax Structure for Property Buying in Italy

The purchase of property in Italy is an involved process that requires a thorough understanding of the associated tax structure. Now we will talk about the detailed tax framework for property acquisition in Italy, with particular emphasis on aspects relevant to foreign buyers. Let's explore key elements of the Italian tax code governing real estate purchases, with provided translations in Italian for major section headers for a comprehensive understanding. Please remember it is alway a great idea to have not only a professional real estate agent to help you, but also an accountant that is familiar how taxes are imposed on expats, and also be able to help your home country

1. Registration Tax (Imposta di Registro)

In Italy, the "Imposta di Registro" refers to the Registration Tax, which is a type of tax imposed on
various legal transactions, including real estate purchases. This tax is a significant component of the

overall costs associated with acquiring property in Italy. The rates and calculations for the Imposta di Registro are based on the fiscal value (valore catastale) that can vary depending on the nature of the property, but it's always lower than the real price.

The rates are applied as follows:

A. Primary Residence:
For individuals purchasing their primary residence, the tax rate is usually lower, 2% of fiscal value.

B. Non-Primary Residence:
For non-primary residences, the tax rates are 9% of fiscal value

C. Luxury Properties:
Luxury properties are buildings of Land Registry Category "Categoria Catastale":

A1. Stately Homes [Abitazioni Signorili]
A8. Villas [Ville]
A9. Castles and Palaces (of particular historical or artistic value [Castelli e Palazzi di particolare pregio storico o artistico]

The tax rates is always 9% of fiscal value even if they are Primary Residence. In other words, you will not have the option to pay a reduced Primary Residence tax rate if you buy a property that is valued as Luxury.

It's important to note that tax laws and rates may be subject to changes, so it is advisable to consult with legal or financial professionals or check the latest regulations to ensure accurate information based on the current date. Additionally, exemptions or reductions may apply in specific cases, such as first-time homebuyers or specific types of properties.

The calculation of the tax is straightforward. It is applied to the declared value of the property transaction. The declared value is the amount stated in the official deed of sale, and it is crucial for buyers to ensure that this value is accurate and reflective of the actual transaction amount. Attempting to declare a lower value to reduce tax liability is illegal and can lead to penalties.

2. Mortgage and Land Registry Tax (Imposta Ipotecaria e Catastale)

In Italy, the Mortgage and Land Registry Tax, known as "Imposta Ipotecaria e Catastale," is a property tax levied on real estate transactions. The tax is applied when registering property deeds with the land registry office. The tax is charged at €50 & €50.? It's essential to consult updated local regulations or seek professional advice for the most accurate information on Imposta Ipotecaria e Catastale rates.

3. Value Added Tax (VAT) - Imposta sul Valore Aggiunto

VAT is applicable to the purchase of NEW constructions in Italy if bought directly from the builder of the property. Think of it as a sales tax… The standard percentage is 10%, but it might vary based on different circumstances, such as the intended use of the property. Foreign buyers should pay particular attention to this tax as it can contribute significantly to the overall cost. There are certain variations in the imposition of the tax. If the property for sale was built over 48 months prior to the sale and had never been sold before, there should no longer be any VAT tax charged on it.

4. Local Property Tax (Imposta Municipale Unica - IMU)

The local property tax (ICI), now merged into the Unique Municipal Tax (IMU), is another significant component of the tax burden for property owners in Italy. This tax is based on the cadastral value of the property and may vary depending on the location.

Imposta Municipale Unica (IMU) is the Local Property Tax in Italy, introduced in 2012 to replace the previous property tax system. IMU is levied on the ownership of real estate and applies to residential and commercial properties. The tax is collected by local municipalities, providing them with a crucial source of revenue.

IMU rates can vary based on property type, location, and usage. The standard IMU rate for primary residences is 0.76%, while secondary residences and agricultural land may have higher rates. Luxury properties, such as villas with pools, may face additional surcharges.

Local authorities have the autonomy to adjust IMU rates within certain limits, leading to variations across regions in Italy. Additionally, municipalities can grant deductions or exemptions to specific categories of properties or residents. Normally, there is no IMU tax on primary residences.

It's important to note that changes to IMU rates and regulations may occur, so consulting updated local legislation or seeking advice from tax professionals is recommended.

IMU is calculated based on the cadastral value of the property, which is an assessed value used for tax purposes.

This value is determined by the land registry office and may differ significantly from the market value. Property owners typically receive an annual IMU notice from their municipality detailing the amount due and the payment deadline.

Failure to pay IMU on time may result in penalties, including interest charges and potential legal actions. Therefore, property owners in Italy should stay informed about local regulations, regularly check for updates, and ensure compliance with IMU obligations. Normally IMU is not charged on

5. Capital Gains Tax on Real Estate (Plusvalenza sugli Immobili)

Capital gains tax on real estate applies when selling a property at a price higher than the purchase price. For foreigners, understanding the tax implications of a future sale is crucial. Currently, the rate is 26%, but it varies based on different factors. If you have lived in the property you are selling for the majority of the time you have owned it, you will probably not be liable for Capital Gains tax on the sale. There is no Capital Gains tax on property you have owned for more than 60 months when you sell it. If you are selling a property in another country, and if you have declared tax residency in Italy, you may be liable for capital gains on those sales depending on certain factors. It is very important to engage a competent Italian tax accountant if you are planning on moving or selling assets while in Italy regardless of their location.

6. Special Tax Regime for Foreign Residents (Regime Fiscale Agevolato per Residenti Esteri)

Foreigners deciding to become tax residents in Italy can benefit from a special tax regime. This regime entails favorable taxation on foreign income and might make Italy a more attractive option for those intending to purchase property and settle in the country. There is a tax plan for example for retirees that are willing to settle in Southern Italy, with certain limitations on size of villages and other factors. For Example, the "7%" plan is enforce at the time of writing. It will set the tax rate on foreign pensions at a flat 7%, much lower than the 23-43% tax you might otherwise pay. Plans of the government can and do often change in Italy. Check with your various professionals and also online for the most current updates!

7. Income Declaration and Tax Obligations (Dichiarazione dei Redditi e Obblighi Fiscali)

Foreign buyers must be aware of the tax obligations associated with property ownership in Italy. They need to regularly file income declarations and fulfill all other tax obligations as per Italian law. Local tax and legal advice can be invaluable to ensure compliance with all obligations.

Purchasing property in Italy as a foreigner requires a comprehensive understanding of the complex Italian tax structure. From registration tax to VAT, through IMU and capital gains tax, each aspect must be carefully considered. Understanding these elements is crucial to avoid financial surprises and ensure that the acquisition of property in Italy is a profitable investment. Expert tax and legal advice are strongly recommended to ensure that foreign buyers meet all their tax obligations in accordance with Italian legislation.

Chapter 8

MAINTENANCE & RENOVATIONS

BEST PRACTICES FOR CARING FOR YOUR REAL ESTATE PURCHASE

Understanding Historical Property Maintenance in Italy

The very first property that I bought in Italy was a 500 year old large apartment in Palazzo Buratti in Montepulciano, Tuscany. It was actually a set of three apartments that spanned over 300 square meters or roughly 3,000 square feet. I remember the day that I got the key to the apartment. It was the biggest key I had ever had and of course it didn't even fit on my keychain. I bought this apartment knowing that we would have a very serious job in front of us to bring the apartment up to 21st century standards. In addition to replacing a total of 5 bathrooms, we needed to add 2 AC systems, completely gut the kitchen, put in all new flooring, paint the entire property and more!

Like everywhere, the total cost of the project exceeded the projection and of course the time it took was much longer than I expected. The funny thing was that everybody here thought we had preformed miracles that it only took 12 months to rehab the apartment while I thought it had taken twice as long as it should have!

Property maintenance is a critical aspect of real estate ownership, and in Italy, this significance is amplified, particularly when it comes to historical buildings. Italy boasts a rich cultural and architectural heritage, with a myriad of historical structures that contribute to its unique charm. The upkeep of these buildings is essential not only for preserving their aesthetic and historical value but also for ensuring the safety and functionality of these assets.

Historical buildings in Italy are often characterized by intricate designs, age-old craftsmanship, and cultural significance, require meticulous maintenance to safeguard their integrity. Preservation efforts play a crucial role in retaining the authenticity and character of these structures, which are not only valuable assets but also integral components of the nation's cultural identity.

One of the primary reasons for emphasizing property maintenance in Italy, particularly for historical buildings, is the preservation of cultural heritage. Italy is home to a plethora of historical sites, including ancient ruins, medieval castles, Renaissance palaces, and Baroque churches. These structures represent different epochs of art, architecture, and history, attracting tourists and scholars alike. Neglecting the maintenance of these buildings could lead to irreversible damage, resulting in the loss of cultural treasures that contribute significantly to Italy's global standing as a cradle of civilization.

Moreover, historical buildings are often constructed using traditional materials and techniques that may not be prevalent in contemporary construction. The conservation of these structures requires specialized knowledge and skills. Preservation efforts involve not only routine maintenance tasks but also the use of
traditional materials and craftsmanship to ensure that any repairs or renovations align with the original construction methods. This commitment to authenticity not only contributes to the longevity of the buildings but also promotes the continuation of traditional craftsmanship, supporting local artisans and preserving cultural techniques.

In addition to cultural considerations, property maintenance is essential for ensuring the safety and structural integrity of historical buildings. Many of these structures have stood for centuries, facing various environmental challenges such as earthquakes, floods, and exposure to the elements. Regular inspections and maintenance activities, including repairs to structural elements, roofs, and facades, are imperative to mitigate the impact of these factors. Neglecting maintenance could lead to serious structural issues, compromising the safety of occupants and visitors.

The economic importance of property maintenance in Italy cannot be understated, especially concerning historical buildings. Tourism is a significant contributor to the Italian economy, and historical sites are among the primary attractions for visitors. Well-maintained buildings enhance the overall visitor experience,
attracting more tourists and contributing to the economic development of the surrounding regions. Conversely, neglecting maintenance could result in a decline in tourism, negatively impacting the local economy and diminishing the value of the historical assets.

Furthermore, the maintenance of historical properties often involves collaboration between public and private entities. Government bodies, cultural institutions, and private property owners need to work together to ensure the sustained upkeep of these buildings. Government initiatives, grants, and regulations may encourage property owners to invest in maintenance activities, fostering a collective responsibility for preserving Italy's cultural heritage.

Beyond the preservation of cultural and economic assets, property maintenance in Italy is vital for environmental sustainability. Historic buildings are part of the ecological landscape, and maintaining them with eco-friendly practices contributes to overall sustainability efforts. The use of environmentally friendly materials, energy-efficient systems, and sustainable conservation practices aligns with global efforts to reduce the environmental impact of human activities. By integrating sustainable practices into property maintenance, Italy can showcase a commitment to environmental responsibility while preserving its historical legacy.

The importance of property maintenance in Italy, especially for historical buildings, cannot be overstated. Beyond the immediate benefits of preserving cultural and architectural heritage, property maintenance contributes to economic prosperity, safety, and environmental sustainability. The meticulous care of these historical assets is a testament to Italy's commitment to its rich past and ensures that future generations can continue to appreciate and learn from the nation's unique cultural and architectural legacy.

Finding Reliable Contractors & Suppliers

Embarking on renovation projects in Italy requires careful consideration and meticulous planning, and a crucial aspect of this process is finding appropriate contractors to undertake the work. Whether it's restoring a historic villa, renovating a contemporary apartment, or upgrading a commercial space, choosing the right contractors is fundamental to the success of the project. In Italy, a country renowned for its rich architectural history, the diversity of available contractors reflects the myriad construction needs. Understanding the types of contractors, exploring resources for locating them, and recognizing professional organizations can greatly aid in making informed decisions for successful renovations.

Italy offers a variety of contractors specializing in different aspects of construction and renovation. One of the primary distinctions is between general contractors and specialized contractors. General contractors oversee the entire construction process, managing various subcontractors and ensuring the project's overall coordination. Specialized contractors, on the other hand, focus on specific aspects of construction, such as electrical work, plumbing, or carpentry.

When searching for contractors in Italy, tapping into local resources proves invaluable. Local business directories, both online and print, list a range of contractors along with their contact details and areas of expertise. These directories provide a comprehensive overview of available professionals, aiding in the initial stages of contractor selection.

Word of mouth is another powerful resource for finding reliable contractors. Seeking recommendations from friends, colleagues, or neighbors who have undergone similar renovations can provide valuable insights into the contractors' work quality, professionalism, and adherence to timelines and budgets. Personal referrals often offer a level of trust and assurance that can be challenging to ascertain through other means.

In the digital age, online platforms play a crucial role in connecting property owners with contractors. Websites specializing in construction services, local business directories, and social media platforms can serve as effective tools for researching and contacting potential contractors. Online reviews and testimonials provide additional perspectives on the reputation and performance of contractors, helping prospective clients make informed decisions.

Understanding the different types of contractors and the services they offer is vital when selecting professionals for a renovation project. General contractors, as project managers, oversee the entire construction process, from initial planning to project completion. They coordinate various subcontractors, manage schedules, and ensure that the work aligns with the client's vision and requirements. General contractors are often licensed and experienced in handling diverse projects, making them suitable for comprehensive renovations.

Specialized contractors, on the other hand, focus on specific aspects of construction. Electricians handle electrical systems, plumbers address plumbing needs, and carpenters specialize in woodwork. Masons and tile setters excel in working with stone and tiles, crucial elements in many Italian structures. Specialized contractors bring expertise in their respective fields, ensuring that each aspect of the renovation meets industry standards and regulations.

Architects and architectural firms also play a pivotal role in renovations, especially when dealing with historical buildings. Their expertise in design, preservation, and restoration ensures that the renovation aligns with the architectural integrity of the structure. Engaging an architect can contribute to a cohesive vision for the project and help navigate regulatory requirements for historical properties.

Professional organizations in Italy provide a framework for contractors to enhance their skills, adhere to industry standards, and maintain ethical practices. One such organization is the "Associazione Nazionale Costruttori Edili" (ANCE), the National Association of Building Contractors. ANCE represents the interests of construction companies in Italy, offering a platform for networking, knowledge exchange, and advocacy. Contractors associated with ANCE demonstrate a commitment to professional development and adherence to industry standards.

Another notable organization is the "Ordine degli Architetti, Pianificatori, Paesaggisti e Conservatori" (Order of Architects, Planners, Landscape Architects, and Conservators). This organization represents licensed professionals in the field of architecture and provides a directory of qualified architects. Engaging an architect affiliated with this organization ensures that the professional meets the educational and ethical standards set by the Order.

Additionally, the "Confederazione Nazionale dell'Artigianato" (National Confederation of Crafts) represents artisans and small to medium-sized enterprises in the construction sector. Artisans often play a crucial role in renovations, contributing specialized skills in areas such as stonemasonry, decorative finishes, and traditional craftsmanship. Contractors associated with this confederation demonstrate a commitment to preserving and promoting traditional Italian craftsmanship.

Finding appropriate contractors for renovations in Italy involves a multi-faceted approach. Local resources, such as business directories and personal referrals, provide initial leads. Understanding the different types of contractors and the services they offer is crucial for selecting professionals who align with the project's requirements. Engaging with professional organizations, such as ANCE and the Order of Architects, provides an additional layer of assurance regarding the contractors' qualifications and commitment to industry standards. By combining these resources and considerations, property owners can navigate the complexities of renovation projects in Italy, ensuring successful outcomes that align with their vision and goals

Special note on the following chapters: The size and variations in the Italian real estate market make it impossible to give more than generalities on pricing. In some cases I have given exact pricing data based on personal knowledge of properties I have toured. For the most part, I have given ranges of prices where I can, and a general overview of what may be driving prices in a particular town or region.

Chapter 9

20+ ITALIAN CITIES TO CALL HOME

FROM NORTH TO SOUTH - AMAZING PLACES TO LIVE

LAKE COMO, LOMBARDY

Population: 489,000 (2023, Greater Area)
Elevation: 60 m (194 ft)

Lake Como, nestled in the Lombardy region of northern Italy, is renowned for its breathtaking scenery, charming towns, and rich history. The towns surrounding Lake Como have a fascinating past that dates back centuries, with each one contributing to the region's cultural and architectural heritage.

One of the oldest settlements along the shores of Lake Como is Como itself, the lake's namesake. With a history dating back to Roman times, Como boasts ancient roots that are still visible in its architecture and layout. The town's historical center is adorned with medieval and Renaissance buildings, including the impressive Como Cathedral, which

Bellagio, Lake Como, Lombardy, Italy

took nearly four centuries to complete. Como's strategic location made it a hub for trade and commerce during the Middle Ages, and its prosperity is reflected in the opulence of its historic buildings.

Moving northward along the western shore, one encounters the picturesque town of Cernobbio. Nestled at the foot of the surrounding hills, Cernobbio is known for its elegant villas and gardens. One notable landmark is the Villa d'Este, a Renaissance residence that has been transformed into a luxury hotel. Originally built in the 16th century, the villa showcases the region's architectural grandeur and has hosted numerous historical figures over the centuries.

Varenna, Lake Como, Italy

Bellagio, often referred to as the "Pearl of Lake Como," is situated at the intersection of the lake's three branches. The town's history is marked by its strategic importance, evident in its medieval defensive structures such as the Tower of the Arts. Bellagio's charm lies in its narrow cobblestone streets, historic villas, and vibrant gardens. It has been a favored destination for writers, artists, and nobility seeking inspiration and relaxation.

Varenna, located on the eastern shore of Lake Como, has a history that intertwines with the medieval period. The town features a charming old town center with colorful houses and narrow alleys that lead to the lakefront. Varenna is home to the Villa Monastero, a former Cistercian convent turned noble residence, showcasing both religious and aristocratic influences throughout the centuries.

Heading further north, the town of Menaggio offers a blend of historical and modern elements. Its origins date back to the Roman era, and the town features a variety of architectural styles, including medieval churches and Renaissance palaces. The lakeside promenade and panoramic views of the surrounding mountains add to the town's appeal.

The town of Lecco, located at the southeastern tip of Lake

Boat at Sunset, Lake Como, Italy

Como, has a distinct industrial history. As an important center for iron production during the 19th century, Lecco contributed significantly to the economic development of the region. Today, visitors can explore the historical industrial sites and enjoy the town's lakeside promenade.

The towns surrounding Lake Como have a rich and diverse history that reflects the region's cultural, economic, and architectural evolution. From the ancient roots of Como to the medieval charm of Bellagio, each town contributes to the allure of Lake Como, making it a timeless destination that continues to captivate visitors from around the world.

Lake Como Real Estate Market

The housing market in the Lake Como area has long been a beacon of luxury and sophistication, attracting discerning homebuyers from around the globe. Nestled in the picturesque Lombardy region of northern Italy, Lake Como is renowned for its stunning landscapes, historic villas, and crystal-clear waters. The real estate market in this area reflects the unique blend of natural beauty and cultural richness that defines the region.

One of the key factors driving the demand for housing in the Lake Como area is its exclusive allure. The shores of the lake are dotted with elegant villas, many of which date back to the Renaissance era. These properties often boast meticulously manicured gardens, private docks, and breathtaking views of the surrounding mountains. The charm of Lake Como has not only attracted celebrities and affluent individuals but has also cemented its status as a sought-after destination for high-end real estate investment.

The market dynamics in the Lake Como area have seen a consistent demand for both primary residences and vacation

Shoreline of Lake Como

homes. The region's popularity as a holiday destination, combined with its proximity to Milan and other major cities, makes it an attractive choice for those seeking a tranquil retreat without sacrificing urban conveniences. Additionally, the recent trend towards remote work has contributed to an increased interest in Lake Como as a potential permanent residence, as individuals and families look for idyllic settings that offer a balance between work and leisure.

However, the exclusivity of the Lake Como housing market also translates to higher price points. Properties on the lakefront or those with historical significance command a premium, reflecting the prestige associated with owning real estate in this iconic destination. While the market may experience fluctuations influenced by global economic conditions, the enduring appeal of Lake Como's natural beauty and cultural heritage ensures a resilient and thriving real estate market in the area.

Turin, Piedmont

Population: 843,000 (2023, City)
Metro Area Population 2,200,000 (2023)
Elevation: 239 m (784 ft)

Turin Skyline

Turin is the capital of the Piedmont region in northwest Italy and boasts a rich and interesting history. Settled along the banks of the Po River and surrounded by the majestic Alps, Turin has been witness to the rise and fall of empires, the birth of influential movements, and the flourishing of arts and culture.

The origins of Turin date back to ancient times, with evidence of settlement by the Taurini, a Celtic-Ligurian tribe, as early as the 3rd century BCE. The Romans, recognizing the strategic importance of the area, established a military camp known as Castra Taurinorum around 28 BCE. This marked the beginning of Turin's trajectory as a vital center for trade and administration within the Roman Empire.

Throughout the medieval period, Turin experienced various rulers, including the Lombards and Franks. However, it was under the House of Savoy that Turin emerged as a prominent city. In the 16th century, Emmanuel Philibert, Duke of Savoy, made Turin the capital of the Duchy of Savoy, a move that set the stage for the city's cultural and economic ascendancy.

The 17th century saw Turin undergo a remarkable transformation under the guidance of Christine Marie of France, regent for her young son, Charles Emmanuel II. The city was redesigned by architects such as Ascanio Vitozzi and Carlo di Castellamonte, who created a distinctive urban layout that showcased wide avenues and grand squares. This Baroque influence is still evident in Turin's architecture, with landmarks like the Palazzo Carignano and Palazzo Madama standing as enduring symbols of the era.

Turin's significance continued to grow in the 18th century, especially under the rule of Victor Amadeus II and his successors. The city became a hub of intellectual and artistic activity, attracting luminaries like Voltaire and Rousseau. Additionally, Turin played a pivotal role in the unification of Italy in the 19th century. It was the birthplace of the Risorgimento movement, a political and social revolution that ultimately led to the creation of a unified Italian state in 1861.

The 20th century brought both challenges and triumphs to Turin. It was an industrial powerhouse, known for its automotive industry and the headquarters of Fiat, one of Italy's most iconic companies. However, the city also faced the ravages of World War II, with significant damage inflicted during air raids. In the post-war period, Turin underwent a process of reconstruction and renewal, gradually reclaiming its status as a vibrant cultural and economic center.

Turin's cultural heritage is exemplified by its numerous museums and landmarks. The Museo Egizio, one of the most renowned Egyptian museums outside of Egypt, houses an extensive collection of artifacts. The Mole Antonelliana, originally built as a synagogue, now serves as the National Museum of Cinema and is an iconic symbol of the city's skyline. Turin is also home to the Royal Palace of Turin, a UNESCO World Heritage Site, which served as the residence of the House of Savoy for centuries.

Today, Turin continues to evolve while honoring its historical legacy. The city's commitment to innovation is evident in initiatives like the Turin Smart City project, which focuses on sustainability and technological advancement. Turin remains a cultural hub, hosting events such as the Turin International Book Fair and the Turin Film Festival.

Turin Real Estate Market

The real estate market in Turin is a dynamic landscape. As one of the key cities in the northern region of Italy, Turin has witnessed shifts in its real estate market influenced by global economic trends, urban development initiatives, and the intrinsic value of its historical properties.

Turin's real estate market is characterized by a diverse range of properties that cater to various preferences and needs. The city boasts a mix of historic buildings, modern apartments, and suburban homes, offering potential buyers a broad spectrum of options. The historic city center, with its Baroque and Renaissance architecture, is a focal point for those seeking the charm of cobblestone streets and proximity to cultural landmarks. The demand for properties in these historic districts often leads to a premium on prices, reflecting the scarcity and cultural significance of such real estate.

In recent years, Turin has experienced a surge in urban renewal projects, contributing to the transformation of certain neighborhoods. Areas like the Lingotto district, once an industrial hub, have undergone revitalization, attracting both residential and commercial development. The conversion of the Fiat factory in Lingotto into a multifunctional complex with apartments, offices, and a shopping center is a notable example of adaptive reuse, breathing new life into the urban landscape.

Piazza Vittorio, Turin

Turin's real estate market is also influenced by the city's economic vitality. As a major industrial and economic center, Turin has attracted professionals and businesses, impacting the demand for residential and commercial properties. The presence of multinational corporations, technological startups, and research institutions contributes to a diverse and dynamic real estate environment, with professionals seeking homes near their workplaces and amenities.

The appeal of Turin as a cultural and historical destination has a significant impact on the real estate market. International and domestic buyers often seek properties that reflect the city's architectural heritage, driving demand for residences in well-preserved historical buildings. The demand for such properties extends beyond local buyers, as Turin's global recognition as a UNESCO World Heritage Site and a city with a rich cultural legacy attracts international investors and property enthusiasts.

Turin's real estate market, like many others, has been influenced by broader economic trends. Economic fluctuations, interest rates, and government policies play a role in shaping the market's dynamics. Turin, however, has demonstrated resilience and adaptability, with a real estate sector that continues to evolve in response to changing economic conditions.

In recent years, there has been a growing interest in sustainable and energy-efficient properties, reflecting a global trend toward environmentally conscious living. Developers in Turin are responding to this demand by incorporating eco-friendly features into new constructions and promoting energy-efficient upgrades for existing buildings. This aligns with the city's commitment to sustainability and aligns with the broader Italian and

European initiatives promoting green and sustainable practices in urban development.

Turin's real estate market is a reflection of the city's historical significance, economic vibrancy, and cultural appeal. The diverse range of properties, from historic residences to modern developments, caters to a broad spectrum of buyers. The interplay of historical charm, economic factors, and urban development initiatives positions Turin as a compelling destination for those seeking a unique and dynamic real estate investment.

Milan, Lombardy

Population: 1,354,000 (2023, City)
Metro Area Population 3,200,000 (2023)
Elevation: 120 m (394 ft)

Milan Duomo

Nestled in the heart of Lombardy, Milan stands as a testament to the rich tapestry of history that has woven its way through the city's streets for centuries. As one of Italy's most dynamic and influential cities, Milan's story unfolds like a captivating novel, with each chapter revealing the city's resilience, cultural richness, and evolution.

The origins of Milan can be traced back to ancient times, when it was a Celtic settlement known as Mediolanum. The strategic location of the city, situated on the crossroads of major trade routes, contributed to its early prosperity. In 222 BCE, the Romans conquered Mediolanum, marking the beginning of Milan's long association with Roman rule. The city flourished under Roman influence, becoming a significant center for commerce and culture in the region.

With the fall of the Roman Empire in the 5th century, Milan entered a period of instability. The city experienced the ebb and flow of power as various Germanic tribes and Lombards vied for control. However, it was under the rule of the Lombards in the 6th century that Milan emerged as the capital of the Lombard Kingdom. The Lombards left an indelible mark on the city's architecture and governance, setting the stage for the medieval era.

The medieval period witnessed the rise of powerful families such as the Viscontis and the Sforzas, whose influence shaped Milan's destiny. The iconic Sforza Castle, a symbol of their dominance, stands proudly in the heart of the city. During this time, Milan also played a pivotal role in the Italian Renaissance, with artists like Leonardo da Vinci and Bramante leaving their artistic legacy on the city's landscape.

The 18th century brought significant changes to Milan as it came under Austrian rule. The Habsburgs, who governed the city, left their mark on its architecture and administration. Despite foreign control, Milan continued to be a hub of intellectual and cultural activity, fostering the emergence of Enlightenment ideas that would later contribute to Italy's unification.

Milan, Italy

The 19th century brought about a seismic shift in Milan's history with the Italian unification movement, also known as the Risorgimento. Milan played a pivotal role in this movement, and in 1859, it became part of the newly formed Kingdom of Italy. The unification marked a new chapter in Milan's story, as the city became a beacon of industry and commerce, fueled by the burgeoning textile and manufacturing sectors.

The 20th century brought both triumphs and tribulations to Milan. The city thrived as a cultural and economic powerhouse, hosting the 1906 World Exposition and witnessing the establishment of iconic institutions like La Scala. However, the city also endured the devastating impacts of World War II, with significant damage inflicted during bombings. Milan's post-war recovery was remarkable, and it emerged as a symbol of Italy's reconstruction and economic resurgence.

In the latter half of the 20th century, Milan solidified its reputation as a global fashion and design capital. The emergence of influential designers like Giorgio Armani and Versace, coupled with the establishment of Milan Fashion Week, elevated the city's status on the world stage. Today, Milan is synonymous with style and sophistication, attracting fashion enthusiasts and industry professionals from around the globe.

Refurbished Tram in Milan, Italy

As we traverse the pages of Milan's history, from its humble beginnings as a Celtic settlement to its current status as a global metropolis, one cannot help but marvel at the city's ability to adapt, evolve, and reinvent itself. Milan's journey is a testament to the resilience of its people and the enduring spirit that continues to shape its destiny. From the ancient Roman streets to the modern runways of fashion, Milan remains a city where the past and present converge, creating a narrative that is as diverse and captivating as the city itself.

Milan Real Estate Market

Milan, renowned for its fashion, culture, and historical significance, is not only a global economic hub but also a city with a thriving residential real estate market. In recent years, however, the landscape has undergone significant transformations, particularly in the realm of tourist rentals, reflecting the evolving preferences and demands of both investors and visitors.

Tourist rentals have become a notable facet of Milan's real estate market, with a surge in demand for short-term accommodations fueled by the city's increasing popularity among tourists. The allure of Milan as a fashion and design capital, coupled with its rich cultural heritage, has made it a magnet for travellers seeking immersive experiences. Consequently, property owners have seized the opportunity to cater to this demand, leading to a proliferation of vacation rentals across the city.

One of the notable trends in Milan's residential real estate market is the rise of furnished apartments and serviced residences as preferred choices for short-term stays. These options provide visitors with the comforts of home while offering the flexibility and convenience that traditional hotels may lack. Investors have capitalized on this trend, converting residential units into stylish and fully equipped accommodations that appeal to both leisure and business travellers.

Apartment Ready for Nightly Rentals, Milan Italy

The advent of online platforms, such as Airbnb and Booking.com, has played a pivotal role in shaping the dynamics of Milan's tourist rental market. These platforms have empowered property owners to reach a global audience, facilitating seamless bookings and enhancing the overall visibility of available accommodations. While this has undoubtedly expanded options for visitors, it has also sparked debates about the impact of short-term rentals on the city's housing market, as some argue that the increasing number of tourist rentals may contribute to housing shortages for residents.

In response to these shifting trends, Milan's local authorities have implemented regulatory measures to manage the impact of tourist rentals on the housing market and urban landscape. Stricter regulations on short-term rentals have been introduced to ensure a balance between meeting the needs of tourists and preserving the availability of housing for residents. These regulations aim to address concerns related to the concentration of tourist rentals in certain neighborhoods, potential disruptions to local communities, and the need for fair competition within the hospitality sector.

As Milan navigates the evolving landscape of its residential real estate market, the city finds itself at the intersection of tradition and modernity. The surge in tourist rentals reflects the global appeal of Milan, while the city grapples with the challenges of balancing the interests of property owners, residents, and visitors. With ongoing regulatory efforts and a commitment to sustainable urban development, Milan seeks to maintain its status as a welcoming destination while ensuring the long-term vitality of its residential neighborhoods. The coming years will undoubtedly witness further transformations, as the city continues to adapt to the dynamic forces shaping its real estate landscape.

Verona, Veneto

Population: 255,000 (2023, City)
Elevation: 60 m (194 ft)

From its ancient roots as a Roman colony to its prominence during the Renaissance, Verona has played a crucial role in shaping the cultural and historical tapestry of Italy. However, one of the most enduring and globally recognized elements of Verona's legacy is undoubtedly the timeless love story of Romeo and Juliet.

Romeo and Juliet, Verona Italy

The history of Verona dates back to the Roman Empire when it was established as a colony in the 1st century BC.

Its strategic location along the Adige River made it a vital hub for trade and commerce. Verona flourished as a center of culture and learning, with impressive structures such as the Arena, a well-preserved Roman amphitheater that continues to host events to this day. The city's architectural heritage also includes the Ponte Pietra, a Roman bridge that spans the Adige River, showcasing the enduring engineering prowess of ancient Rome.

Verona's significance continued to evolve through the Middle Ages, as it became a powerful city-state in its own right. The ruling Scaligeri family left an indelible mark on the cityscape, with iconic landmarks like the Scaliger Tombs and the imposing Castelvecchio, a medieval fortress that guarded the city against external threats. Verona's political and economic influence expanded during this period, solidifying its status as a key player in the complex tapestry of Italian city-states.

The Renaissance brought a renewed cultural and artistic flourishing to Verona. The city became a hub for intellectuals and artists, and its architecture reflected the aesthetic ideals of the time. The celebrated painter Paolo Veronese, known for his grandiose works, was among the prominent figures who left their mark on the city during this era. Verona's historic center, with its charming streets and well-preserved buildings, provides a captivating glimpse into this golden age of art and culture.

Despite the city's illustrious history, Verona is perhaps best known globally for the tragic love story of Romeo and Juliet, immortalized by William Shakespeare in the 16th century. While the tale of the star-crossed lovers is fictional, its setting in Verona has transformed the city into a pilgrimage site for lovers and literary enthusiasts alike. The iconic balcony of Juliet's house, a 13th-century residence now known as Casa di Giulietta, draws visitors from around the world seeking to relive the timeless romance. The enduring appeal of Romeo and Juliet lies not only in the tragic narrative but also in the universal themes of love, conflict, and societal expectations. Shakespeare's play has transcended its Elizabethan origins to become a cultural touchstone, influencing countless adaptations, films, and artistic interpretations. Verona's association with this iconic love story has become inseparable from its identity, contributing to the city's allure and international renown.

Verona actively embraces its association with Romeo and Juliet, capitalizing on the literary connection to promote tourism. The city hosts an annual summer festival, the "Verona in Love" celebration, which attracts couples and romantics from all corners of the globe. Visitors can explore Juliet's house, where the walls are adorned with love letters, and the famous balcony stands as a testament to the enduring power of the written word.

The history of Verona is a captivating narrative of evolution, from its Roman roots to its Renaissance glory. The city's architectural wonders and cultural contributions have left an indelible mark on Italy's heritage. However, the tale of Romeo and Juliet has undeniably become a central chapter in Verona's story, elevating the city to a symbol of enduring love and literary significance. Verona stands not only as a testament to the past but also as a living testament to the enduring power of storytelling and the capacity of a city to capture the imagination of the world.

Verona Real Estate Market

The real estate market for apartments in Verona is shaped by two main forces: Tourists accommodations and housing for students that attend the many universities in the area. The University of Verona, founded in 1982, has grown to become a hub of academic excellence with a diverse range of programs across various disciplines. It is known for its commitment to research, innovation, and providing students with a well-rounded education. The university's campus is spread across different locations in the city, offering a blend of modern facilities and historic charm.
One of the notable faculties within the University of Verona is the Faculty of Medicine and Surgery, which has gained recognition for its cutting-edge research and high-quality medical education. The university also boasts strong faculties in humanities, social sciences, natural sciences, engineering, and economics, providing a comprehensive academic experience for students.
Apart from the University of Verona, the city hosts other institutions, including the Conservatory of Music "E. F. Dall'Abaco," offering programs in music and performing arts, and the Verona Academy of Fine Arts, nurturing talent in visual arts.

Over the past few years, Verona has experienced a notable surge in tourist travel, solidifying its position as a must-visit destination. This increase can be attributed to several factors that collectively contribute to the city's growing popularity among travellers.
Efforts to improve infrastructure and accessibility have also played a crucial role in the increased tourism. Verona's well-connected transportation network, including its international

airport and high-speed rail links, makes it easily accessible for travelers from various parts of Europe and beyond.

One of the primary drivers of Verona's tourism boom is its status as a UNESCO World Heritage Site. The city's historic center, with its well-preserved medieval architecture, ancient bridges, and the iconic Arena di Verona, captivates visitors with a journey through time. Verona's cultural richness, reflected in its museums, churches, and Roman ruins, serves as a magnet for history enthusiasts and art aficionados alike.

Arena di Verona

The city's strategic location in the Veneto region, surrounded by the stunning landscapes of Lake Garda and the rolling hills of Valpolicella, further enhances its appeal. Verona acts as a gateway to the diverse attractions of northern Italy, attracting tourists seeking a blend of cultural exploration and natural beauty.

Verona's association with William Shakespeare's timeless love story, "Romeo and Juliet," adds a romantic allure, drawing couples and literature enthusiasts to visit iconic sites like Juliet's House. The annual Verona in Love festival, celebrating Valentine's Day, has become a major attraction, further fueling the city's popularity as a romantic getaway. The city's culinary scene, renowned for its regional specialties like Amarone wine and risotto all'Amarone, contributes to the overall tourist experience. Verona's restaurants, cafes, and local markets offer an authentic taste of Italian gastronomy, making it a gastronomic delight for food enthusiasts.

Verona's surge in tourist travel over the last few years can be attributed to a combination of its UNESCO heritage status, cultural richness, strategic location, romantic associations, improved infrastructure, and delightful culinary offerings. As the city continues to captivate visitors with its unique charm, Verona is poised to remain a prominent destination on the global tourism map.

TREVISO, VENETO

Population: 85,000 (2018, City Proper)
3,000 (within Venetian walls)
Elevation: 15 m (49 ft)

Canals of Treviso

Treviso, a picturesque town in the Veneto region of northeastern Italy, boasts a rich history that unfolds like a tapestry woven with threads of trade, culture, and the indelible influence of its powerful neighbor, Venice. As we delve into the annals of Treviso's past, it becomes evident that its narrative is intricately intertwined with the ebb and flow of commerce, making it a vital player in the economic mosaic of the Venetian Republic.

The origins of Treviso trace back to Roman times when it was known as "Tarvisium." Its strategic location along the Via Claudia Augusta, a major Roman road connecting the Po River with the Adriatic Sea, contributed to its early development as a trading hub. The town's position facilitated the exchange of goods between the fertile Po Valley and the thriving Roman centers along the Adriatic coast.

As the Roman Empire waned, Treviso experienced the tumultuous waves of invasion and conquest that characterized the medieval era. In the 6th century, the Lombards left an indelible mark on the region, but it was the subsequent rule of the Carolingian Empire that laid the foundation for Treviso's emergence as a medieval trading power. The establishment of a market and the construction of defensive walls during this period reflected the town's growing importance in the commercial landscape of northern Italy.

The true turning point in Treviso's history, however, occurred with its integration into the maritime empire of Venice. In the late 12th century, Venice extended its influence over Treviso, bringing the town under its dominion. This marked the beginning of a symbiotic relationship that would significantly shape Treviso's destiny. The Venetians, recognizing the strategic value of Treviso, invested in its infrastructure, fortifications, and, most importantly, its economic potential.

Trade became the lifeblood of Treviso, and its merchants played a pivotal role in the broader Venetian commercial network. The town's proximity to Venice's lagoon and its connection to major trade routes positioned it as a vital link between the inland regions and the maritime trade routes of the Adriatic. Treviso's markets thrived, attracting merchants from across Europe and the Levant.

The Venetian Republic, with its maritime prowess, provided Treviso with unparalleled opportunities for economic growth. The navigable rivers connecting Treviso to the Adriatic Sea facilitated the transportation of goods, allowing the town to flourish as a trading center. Treviso's merchants engaged in the exchange of diverse commodities, including textiles, grains, and the famed Treviso radicchio, a type of chicory that gained regional renown.

The economic success of Treviso was further propelled by its skilled artisans and craftsmen. The town became a hub for the production of high-quality textiles, particularly wool

Prosecco Vineyards Outside of Treviso, Italy

Outdoor Majesty North of Treviso, Veneto, Italy

and silk, which were sought after in markets near and far. The craftsmanship of Treviso became synonymous with luxury and refinement, contributing to the town's affluence.

Treviso's architectural landscape bears witness to its economic prosperity during the Venetian era. Elegant palazzi, adorned with frescoes and intricate details, stand as a testament to the wealth accumulated through trade. The Palazzo dei Trecento, the civic heart of Treviso, exemplifies the grandeur of this period, serving as a gathering place for merchants and a symbol of the town's prosperity.

The Venetian influence also manifested in the urban planning of Treviso. Canals, reminiscent of those in Venice, crisscrossed the town, facilitating transportation and trade. The Venetians brought their expertise in hydraulic engineering to Treviso, transforming it into a town that mirrored the beauty and functionality of its maritime neighbor.

The decline of the Venetian Republic in the late 18th century had a profound impact on Treviso. The Napoleonic invasion and subsequent Austrian rule altered the political landscape, reshaping the dynamics of trade in the region. However, the legacy of Treviso's mercantile past endured, leaving an imprint on the town's identity that is still visible today.

Treviso's history is a narrative woven with the threads of trade and the enduring influence of Venice. From its early days as a Roman trading post to its golden age as a key player in the Venetian commercial network, Treviso's story mirrors the rise and fall of empires. As one strolls through the charming streets of Treviso, it is impossible to escape the echoes of its mercantile past, a testament to the enduring legacy of trade in shaping the town's destiny.

Treviso Real Estate Market

The real estate market in Treviso is experiencing a notable surge in popularity and growth, driven by various factors that contribute to its appeal as a desirable location. Situated in the Veneto region, Treviso boasts a rich cultural heritage, historic charm, and proximity to the renowned city of Venice.

One of the key drivers behind the burgeoning real estate market in Treviso is the increasing influx of tourists to the region. Treviso has gradually emerged as a sought-after destination for travellers seeking an authentic Italian experience away from the bustling crowds of major tourist

Grand Canal, Venice Italy

hubs. The city's well-preserved medieval architecture, picturesque canals, and vibrant local culture make it an attractive option for those looking to explore the beauty of Northern Italy.

The strategic proximity to Venice further enhances Treviso's appeal, as it allows residents and visitors easy 30 minute access by train to one of the world's most iconic and enchanting cities. Venice, known for its historic canals, intricate architecture, and cultural richness, is just a short distance away from Treviso. This close proximity not only adds to the cultural allure of living in Treviso but also opens up numerous opportunities for day trips and exploration.

As the tourism industry continues to thrive in the region, the real estate market in Treviso benefits from increased demand for accommodation options. Investors and homeowners alike are capitalizing on the growing interest in the area, contributing to a robust real estate market. The demand for vacation rentals, in particular, has seen a significant uptick, as visitors seek unique and authentic experiences beyond the standard hotel stay.

However, with the rise in popularity of short-term rentals, local authorities in Treviso have implemented regulations to manage the impact on the housing market and maintain the city's character. Nightly rental regulations aim to strike a balance between meeting the needs of tourists and preserving the residential fabric of the city. These regulations often include restrictions on the number of days a property can be rented per year and requirements for obtaining proper permits.

For homeowners and investors interested in the Treviso real estate market, it is crucial to navigate these regulations to ensure compliance and avoid potential legal issues. Engaging with local authorities and understanding the specific rules governing nightly rentals is essential for those looking to participate in the growing tourism-driven economy.

As the city continues to attract both visitors and investors, it is essential for stakeholders to be aware of and adhere to regulations governing nightly rentals to ensure sustainable growth and the preservation of Treviso's distinctive character. The combination of cultural richness, historical significance, and a thriving tourism industry positions Treviso as a compelling destination for those looking to invest in Italian real estate.

Venice, Veneto

**Population: 125,000 (2022)
Elevation: 1 m (3 ft)**

Saint Marks Square, Venice, Italy

Nestled on the shores of the Adriatic Sea, Venice, Italy, is a city of enchanting waterways, magnificent architecture, and a rich historical tapestry. Its unique setting, with a network of canals serving as its streets, has earned it the nickname "The Floating City." The history of Venice is a captivating narrative that spans over a millennium, shaped by its maritime prowess, cultural achievements, and enduring allure to tourists.

Venice's origins can be traced back to the 5th century AD when inhabitants of the mainland sought refuge on the marshy islands of the Venetian Lagoon to escape barbarian invasions. The city's foundation is often attributed to the establishment of the first church, San Giacomo di Rialto, in 421 AD. Over the centuries, Venice evolved into a powerful maritime republic, fostering trade, diplomacy, and cultural exchange with the East and the West.

Carnival, Venice, Italy

During the Middle Ages and the Renaissance, Venice flourished as a major trading hub, accumulating wealth through commerce, shipbuilding, and banking. The city-state became a center of art and culture, nurturing iconic figures such as Titian, Tintoretto, and Vivaldi. The construction of elegant palaces, grand churches, and the iconic St. Mark's

Basilica showcased Venice's architectural splendor, contributing to its reputation as a beacon of opulence.

Gondolier on Grand Canal, Venice, Italy

The Venetian Republic, with its unique system of governance and a powerful navy, maintained its independence for centuries. However, the city's fortunes began to decline in the late 17th century due to a combination of military defeats, economic challenges, and the changing dynamics of global trade routes. Nevertheless, Venice's cultural legacy endured, leaving an indelible mark on the world.

In the 19th century, Venice became part of the newly formed Kingdom of Italy, marking the end of the Venetian Republic. The city continued to captivate artists, writers, and intellectuals who were drawn to its romantic ambiance and historical grandeur. By the turn of the 20th century, Venice had firmly established itself as a cultural and artistic hub, attracting tourists seeking to experience the city's unique charm.

The advent of mass tourism in the mid-20th century brought a new chapter in Venice's history. The city's timeless allure and architectural treasures became accessible to a broader audience, and Venice embraced its role as a premier tourist destination. The Grand Canal, St. Mark's Square, and the Rialto Bridge became iconic landmarks drawing millions of visitors each year.

Grand Canal and Cathedral, Venice, Italy

Tourism has played a dual role in shaping Venice's contemporary identity. On one hand, it has injected economic vitality into the city, supporting businesses, preservation efforts, and cultural institutions. On the other hand, the sheer volume of tourists has presented challenges, including concerns about environmental impact, preservation of historical sites, and the balance between the needs of residents and the demands of visitors.

The historic center of Venice was inscribed on the UNESCO World Heritage List in 1987, acknowledging its unique urban structure and cultural significance. However, the city has grappled with issues such as overcrowding, the impact of large cruise ships, and the effects of high water (aqua alta) due to rising sea levels. Efforts have been made to implement sustainable tourism practices, regulate visitor numbers, and address the environmental challenges faced by the city.

Venice continues to be a beacon for cultural enthusiasts, history lovers, and romantics alike. The city's festivals, including the famous Carnival of Venice, draw visitors from around the world, contributing to its reputation as a year-round destination. Despite the complexities posed by modern tourism, Venice remains an unparalleled marvel, inviting travelers to immerse themselves in its timeless beauty, explore its winding canals, and discover the rich layers of history that have shaped this extraordinary city.

Venice Real Estate Market

Venice from Rental Apartment Window

Venice, with its unique charm and historical significance, has been a popular destination for tourists, leading to a surge in the demand for short-term rental properties. To regulate this growing market and address concerns related to the impact of tourism on the city, Venice implemented variousregulations.

One significant regulation focuses on short-term rentals, which gained popularity through platforms like Airbnb. The city introduced measures to curb the negative effects of mass tourism on the local housing market and the overall quality of life for residents. As of 2022, property owners looking to engage in short-term rentals were required to adhere to specific guidelines.

One of the key regulations was the necessity for property owners to obtain proper licenses for short-term rentals. This process involved meeting certain criteria, such as ensuring the property met safety standards and compliance with zoning regulations. Failure to obtain the necessary licenses could result in fines and penalties.

Venice Italy

Additionally, there were restrictions on the number of days a property could be rented out as a short-term rental. These limitations aimed to strike a balance between accommodating tourists and preserving the availability of housing for local residents. It was crucial for property owners to stay informed about these regulations to avoid legal complications.

Grand Canal, Venice

Furthermore, in an effort to manage the impact of tourism on the city's infrastructure and services, Venice implemented a tourist tax. The tax, applicable to both overnight visitors and day-trippers, contributed to the maintenance and improvement of the city. The amount of the tax varied depending on factors such as the type of accommodation, the time of year, and the duration of the stay.

The tourist tax was seen as a way to mitigate the strain on Venice's resources caused by the influx of visitors. Funds collected from the tax were allocated to initiatives that aimed to preserve the city's cultural heritage, maintain public spaces, and support sustainable tourism practices.

It is essential to note that regulations and policies can change, and the information provided is based on the situation as of 2022. For the most up-to-date information on the real estate market, short-term rental regulations, and tourist taxes in Venice, it is recommended to consult local authorities, official government websites, or reliable news sources.

Prices for properties in Venice are very elevated due to the huge influx of tourists. On par with Florence and Rome, it is easy to spend €5,000/MQ ($550/sq ft) for prime apartments in Venice. As always, apartments with views of the Grand Canal, or terraces will command even higher prices.

Lucca, Tuscany

Population: 89,000 (2023)
Lucca Province Population 383,000 (2023)
Elevation: 19 m (62 ft)

Lucca, a charming city in Tuscany, Italy, boasts a rich history that spans thousands of years, with significant developments during the Roman and Middle Ages. Its strategic location and flourishing trade played crucial roles in shaping the city's identity.

Lucca, Italy

The Roman era marked Lucca's initial rise to prominence. Originally settled by the Etruscans, Lucca became a Roman colony around 180 BCE. The Romans recognized the strategic value of Lucca's location, situated on the crossroads of important trade routes and surrounded by fertile plains. The city thrived as a hub for commerce, agriculture, and craftsmanship.

The ancient walls stand as an enduring testament to the city's historical significance and strategic importance. Constructed during the Roman era in the 2nd century CE, these well-preserved fortifications have played a crucial role in shaping the city's identity. The walls served as a formidable defense mechanism against external threats, reflecting the strategic foresight of the Romans who recognized Lucca's geographical importance at the crossroads of major trade routes.

During the Middle Ages, when political upheavals and conflicts were commonplace in Italy, Lucca's walls provided a sense of security and allowed the city to maintain its autonomy. The imposing structure not only shielded the city from potential invasions but also served as a symbol of Lucca's resilience and determination to safeguard its economic and cultural prosperity.

In addition to their defensive function, the walls became a defining feature of Lucca's urban landscape. Over time, the city expanded within the confines of the fortifications, and the walls evolved into a unique promenade. Today, they offer residents and visitors alike a scenic pathway to explore Lucca's historic center while preserving the city's charm and architectural heritage. The walls of Lucca remain a living testament to the city's rich history, standing tall as both a protective barrier and a symbol of endurance through the ages.

Trade flourished during the Middle Ages, and Lucca emerged as a key player in the region's economic landscape. The city's merchants engaged in trade across the Mediterranean, contributing to its prosperity. Lucca's geographical position allowed it to establish connections with other major Italian cities, as well as with ports in the Byzantine Empire and North Africa.

One of the most significant economic activities during the Middle Ages was the production of high-quality silk. Lucca became renowned for its silk industry, and the city's silk products were highly sought after in international markets. The silk trade brought immense wealth to Lucca, contributing to the construction of impressive churches, palaces, and public buildings that still stand today.

Piazza dell'Antiteatro, Lucca, Italy

Lucca's thriving trade network also played a role in its political and cultural development. The city became a prominent center for banking and finance, with influential families like the Guinigi and the Puccinelli contributing to the city's economic and political landscape. These families commissioned renowned artists and architects to create masterpieces that enriched Lucca's cultural heritage.

Church of San Michele, Lucca, Italy

During the Middle Ages, Lucca was not immune to the power struggles that characterized the Italian peninsula. The city experienced periods of both independence and subjugation to larger regional powers. Its ability to maintain a delicate balance between alliances and independence allowed Lucca to safeguard its economic interests and cultural achievements.

The city's commitment to maintaining its autonomy is evident in its well-preserved urban fabric, with narrow streets, medieval towers, and elegant palaces. Lucca's commitment to self-governance was a testament to its resilience and determination to preserve its unique identity in the face of external pressures.

Lucca's history during the Roman and Middle Ages is a testament to its strategic importance as a center for trade and commerce. The city's geographical location, combined with its economic activities such as silk production, contributed to its prosperity and cultural richness. Lucca's ability to navigate political challenges and preserve its autonomy allowed it to leave an indelible mark on the history of Tuscany and Italy as a whole. The remnants of its Roman walls and medieval architecture stand as tangible evidence of a city that has weathered the centuries, maintaining its charm and allure to this day.

Lucca Real Estate Market

The historic center of Lucca, Italy stands as a testament to the city's rich cultural heritage, drawing tourists from around the globe with its timeless allure. Enclosed by well-preserved Renaissance walls, the heart of Lucca transports visitors to an enchanting world where cobblestone streets wind their way through a maze of medieval and Renaissance architecture.

The appeal of Lucca's historic center lies not only in its architectural splendor but also in its intimate, welcoming atmosphere. Visitors are encouraged to explore hidden

The Walls of Lucca, Italy

corners, discover quaint trattorias, and savor the authentic flavors of Tuscan cuisine. This blend of history, culture, and gastronomy creates an irresistible magnetism, making Lucca's historic center a must-visit destination for those seeking an immersive experience in the heart of Italy's cultural tapestry.

Properties that are within the city walls can be 100% or more expensive than a similar property outside of the walls, and the reason is simply the tastes of tourists that come here and where they want to stay. A three bedroom apartment outside the city walls that is in great shape and only a 600 meter walk to the historic center might be €160,000. That same property would be well over €500,000, if not more in the historic center.

In the past, most cities in Italy had a very predictable season for tourists, normally running from late spring to autumn.

Now cities that are among the most popular can see almost year round rentals to the tourist trade, and this is pushing up pricing in those areas. Lucca is a great case in point. The average price for a good quality apartment within the Historic Center of Lucca has gone up about 30% on average over the last four years according to local real estate agents. Italy in general is not known for its price appreciation, but in many of the most popular tourist towns this is exactly what is happening.

Outside of Lucca there are many towns in the hills and valleys within 20 miles. Most of the towns do not have the high price tag that the historic center of Lucca has. A 4,000 sq ft home in great shape with a view and private parking can cost as little as €300,000! Smaller apartments can be had for under €100,000 in most townships.

Overall, Lucca is one of the strongest rental markets in Italy for the tourist trade. If you are thinking about buying investment properties you could do very well in Lucca if you buy at the right price and with the correct amenities. Remember that tourists that are renting will be looking for the same things that you might want in your apartment or home. Buying an apartment that you can both enjoy and lease on the nightly rental market will give you an additional buffer in case your living plans change.

Pisa, Tuscany

Population: 98,000 (2023)
Elevation: 4 m (13 ft)

Pisa, a picturesque city in Tuscany, Italy, has a rich and diverse history that spans over many centuries. From its humble beginnings as a Roman settlement to its rise as a maritime power and cultural center, Pisa has played a significant role in shaping the history of Italy and beyond.

Leaning Tower of Pisa

The origins of Pisa date back to ancient times when it was initially settled by the Ligurians, an ancient Indo-European people, around the 5th century BC. However, it was the Romans who established Pisa as a strategically important port city, connecting the region to the rest of the Roman Empire. The city thrived as a trade center and played a crucial role in the Roman maritime activities.

As the Roman Empire declined, Pisa went through a period of instability and was later conquered by various barbarian tribes. In the 9th century, Pisa began to reemerge as a significant player in the region. It became a maritime republic and started expanding its influence through trade and military power. The construction of the Pisa Cathedral, dedicated to St. Mary of the Assumption, began in 1064 and marked the city's commitment to establishing itself as a cultural and religious center.

Pisa's golden age reached its peak in the 12th century when it became a major naval power in the Mediterranean. The city's fleet engaged in trade with the Byzantine Empire, North Africa, and the Middle East, accumulating wealth and cultural influences. Pisa's maritime prowess was exemplified by the construction of the iconic Leaning Tower of Pisa, which started in 1173. The tower, initially intended to be a freestanding bell tower for the cathedral, gained fame due to its unintended tilt caused by unstable foundation soil. However, the prosperity of Pisa was short-lived. In the 13th century, conflicts with Genoa, Venice, and other Italian city-states led to a decline in Pisa's maritime influence. The Battle of Meloria in 1284, where the Pisan fleet suffered a devastating defeat against Genoa, marked the end of Pisa's naval dominance.

Pisa's decline did not halt its cultural contributions. The University of Pisa, founded in 1343, became a renowned

Arno River in Pisa, Italy

center for learning during the Renaissance. Figures like Galileo Galilei, a pioneering scientist, taught and conducted research at the university in the 16th and 17th centuries. Over the centuries, Pisa went through periods of occupation and change. The city experienced architectural and cultural revivals during the Renaissance and Baroque eras, leaving a lasting impact on its urban landscape. In the 19th century, Pisa played a role in the Italian unification process and became part of the Kingdom of Italy in 1860.

Today, Pisa is globally recognized for its iconic leaning tower, Piazza dei Miracoli, and its historical significance. The city's blend of Romanesque and Gothic architecture, along with its academic heritage, attracts millions of tourists each year. Pisa's history reflects its resilience, cultural contributions, and the enduring charm that continues to captivate visitors from around the world.

Pisa Real Estate Market

Pisa is often thought of as a "one night stand" for travelers. The reality is that Pisa is a great place to have as a base for traveling and exploring for either a few days or as your permanent home. Pisa is near to Cinque Terre, the Beaches of Northern Tuscany, the ferry services of Livorno and of course only 20 minutes from Lucca. It is served by a major airport with direct flights to many European capitals. Like all major Italian cities, Pisa is served by high speed rail service that can have you in Rome in just a few hours.

The real estate market in Pisa is not as red hot as some of its other neighbours in Tuscany like Lucca and Florence. However, the cost of apartments and homes reflects this difference which can make Pisa an affordable alternative to the other major players in tourism which is the main driver of prices in Italy.

Apartments for long term rental can range from €400-1000/month. Long term rental period is usually from 1-3 years with renewals for another 1-3 years after that. Short term but low cost rentals are usually not available. Sometimes you can find "Winter Months" specials here for rentals near the beach that are quite reasonable, but only available from November to March more or less. Those rental rates can be excellent and the apartment are usually furnished.

Homes in Pisa can range from $200-400 per square foot for nice apartments and homes. Of course location is everything and some homes can be much more per square foot.

FLORENCE, TUSCANY

**Population: 361,000 (2023)
Elevation: 50 m (164 ft)**

Florence, Italy

Florence, the capital city of the Italian region of Tuscany, boasts a rich and storied history that spans over a millennium. The city's origins can be traced back to Roman times when it was established as a settlement for retired soldiers in the 1st century BCE. Known as Florentia, the city flourished as a hub for trade and commerce due to its strategic location along the Roman road known as the Via Cassia.

During the Middle Ages, Florence evolved into a powerful and influential city-state. The rise of powerful families, such as the Medici, played a pivotal role in shaping Florence's destiny. The Medici family, a dynasty of bankers, merchants, and patrons of the arts, rose to prominence in the 15th century and became the de facto rulers of the city. Lorenzo de' Medici, also known as Lorenzo the Magnificent, was a key figure in fostering the Renaissance, a period of cultural and artistic rebirth that swept across Europe.

The Renaissance marked a golden age for Florence, as the city became a center of artistic, literary, and scientific achievements. Artists like Leonardo da Vinci, Michelangelo, and Botticelli, who were sponsored by the Medici family, produced masterpieces that are celebrated to this day. Florence's architectural landscape was also transformed during this period, with landmarks like Brunelleschi's Dome of the Florence Cathedral and the Palazzo Medici Riccardi standing as testaments to the city's cultural flourishing.

Despite its cultural achievements, Florence was not immune to political turmoil. The struggle for power and influence led to conflicts between rival factions, resulting in episodes like the Pazzi Conspiracy in 1478, which targeted the Medici family but ultimately failed. The Medici, however, managed to maintain their dominance for several centuries, until the last Medici ruler died without a male heir in 1737.

Following the decline of Medici rule, Florence experienced a series of political changes. It became part of the Grand Duchy of Tuscany under the Habsburg-Lorraine dynasty and later aligned with the Kingdom of Italy in the 19th century. The city played a crucial role in the Italian unification movement, which culminated in 1861 with the establishment of the Kingdom of Italy. Florence briefly served as the capital of the newly unified Italy before the seat of government was moved to Rome.

Florence Duomo

In the 20th century, Florence faced challenges during World War II when it fell under German occupation. The city suffered significant damage due to Allied bombings, leading to the destruction of numerous historical buildings and artworks. However, post-war reconstruction efforts focused on restoring Florence's cultural heritage, and the city regained its status as a global cultural center.

Today, Florence stands as a testament to its rich history, with its well-preserved medieval and Renaissance architecture attracting millions of visitors each year. The historic center, a UNESCO World Heritage site, encompasses landmarks such as the Uffizi Gallery, Ponte Vecchio, and the Florence Cathedral, showcasing the city's enduring cultural legacy. Florence continues to be a thriving center for the arts, education, and commerce, embodying a harmonious blend of its ancient past and modern vitality. The city's legacy as the birthplace of the Renaissance and a cradle of creativity ensures its enduring significance on the world stage.

Florence Real Estate Market

Florence, renowned for its historical charm and cultural significance, has historically been an attractive destination for real estate investment. The city's real estate market has been characterized by a mix of historical properties, such as Renaissance palaces and medieval buildings, as well as more modern developments. The demand for real estate in Florence is often driven not only by locals but also by international buyers seeking a piece of the city's rich history.

Bridges, Florence, Italy

One notable aspect of Florence's real estate market is the preservation and restoration efforts associated with its historic properties. The city has stringent regulations to ensure the conservation of its architectural heritage. This has led to a unique market where restored historical properties coexist with more contemporary housing options. The limited availability of historical properties and the restrictions on modifications contribute to their desirability, often making them a sought-after investment.

Tourism has long been a significant factor influencing Florence's real estate market. The city's popularity as a tourist destination has led to a market for short-term rentals, such as vacation apartments. Changes in tourism patterns or regulations regarding short-term rentals can have an impact on the local housing market.

Additionally, urban development projects and infrastructure improvements can influence property values and demand in specific neighborhoods. Florence, with its commitment to preserving its historical character, carefully navigates the balance between modernization and conservation.

The nightly rental market for tourists is the driving force for pricing in the real estate market in Florence. The rental market in Florence for nightly rentals is virtually 365 days a year. It's a very important distinction from many other cities where the average rental is only in use 200 to 240 days a year, or in some seasonal rentals like beaches or ski resorts the rental needs can be as low as 100 nights per year. Very few cities in Italy can boost this type of rental optimisation… only Lucca, Rome, and Venice even come close.

The cost of buying apartments in Florence inside the historic centre, can range from €4,000 to €9,000 per square meter or roughly $500-$1000 per square foot for prime properties.

In the outlying areas, you can find properties that are much less expensive, but the really high end rentals that are going to rented year round are going to be inside the historic center and within walking distance to major attractions. Within 20 minutes of Florence, you can find apartments for sale that are less than 20% of this price. You will be able to find apartments under €75,000 that are a 20 minute tram ride into the city centre proper. You will also be able to find 1,200 square-foot homes for well under a $200,000. As it the case everywhere, price is dictated by location, location, location…

San Gimignano, Tuscany

Population: 7,480 (2023)
Elevation: 324 m (1,063 ft)

Nestled in the heart of Tuscany, San Gimignano stands as a living testament to medieval charm and architectural ingenuity. This small, walled town is renowned for its well-preserved towers, which pierce the sky and dominate the picturesque skyline, earning it the moniker "The Town of Fine Towers." The history of San Gimignano is a tale that unfolds through the centuries, reflecting the ebbs and flows of political power, economic prosperity, and cultural dynamism.

Towers, San Gimignano, Italy

San Gimignano's origins can be traced back to ancient times when it served as a stopping point for pilgrims and travelers on the Via Francigena, an important medieval pilgrimage route from Canterbury to Rome. During the Middle Ages, the town began to flourish as a center of trade and commerce, strategically positioned along routes connecting northern Europe to Rome and the Mediterranean. Its elevated position atop a hill provided both strategic advantages and breathtaking views of the surrounding countryside.

The town's defining feature, its towers, emerged as a symbol of wealth and power. Families vied with each other to construct taller and more extravagant towers, creating a unique skyline that reflected the social hierarchy of the time. At its peak in the 13th century, San Gimignano boasted around 72 towers, each serving as a testament to the prosperity of its noble families.

As with many medieval towns in Italy, San Gimignano faced the challenges of political turbulence. It was a free commune for much of its early history, but in the 12th century, it fell under the influence of the Bishop of Volterra. The struggle for autonomy and control played out over the centuries, involving various factions and external powers.

The 14th century brought its own set of challenges, as the Black Death swept through Europe, causing a devastating loss of life. San Gimignano, like many other communities, felt the impact of this pandemic, leading to a decline in population and economic activity. The subsequent economic downturn also marked the beginning of the end for the town's prominence as a major trade hub.

City View, San Gimignano, Italy

By the Renaissance, San Gimignano had settled into a more provincial role, and the towers that once symbolized wealth became obsolete. The town's economic decline paradoxically contributed to the preservation of its medieval character, as there was little incentive for modernization or expansion.

In the 19th century, San Gimignano experienced a renewal of interest and appreciation, thanks in part to the Romantic movement that sought to rediscover and celebrate the beauty of medieval and Renaissance Italy. Artists and writers drew inspiration from the town's unique architecture, and efforts were made to restore and protect its historical monuments.

San Gimignano Real Estate Market

San Gimignano has become a very popular destination for wine lovers where you can spend one or two nights on trips out of Florence travelling through Tuscany. The town is rather small with a population of only about 2000 people inside the historic center. The town receives a large amount of tourist traffic, more than one million people a year. Most are day trippers, but some people decide to spend one or two nights while enjoying the surrounding area for wine tours and site seeing to enjoy the Tuscan countryside.

Home prices in the town mirror those in another southern Tuscany towns like Siena. The historic center is not large so the overall number of rental properties versus the huge number of tourist keeps property prices at a premium.

In the current market you can expect to pay €300,000+ for a nice two bedroom one bath apartment. Of course it's very hard to find an independent home inside the historic district, but outside you can find country homes, call "casale", with starting prices in the €600,000 range for something with a little land and that is in good condition.

Remember that it's important to always research very thoroughly the market conditions if you're planning on renting to the tourist trade. Many cities have some regulations in place that may limit what you can do with a particular apartment.

Montepulciano, Tuscany

Population: 13,200 (2023)
Elevation: 605 m (1,984 ft)

Montepulciano, Siena, Tuscany

Its origins can be traced back to ancient times, and its development reflects the intricate tapestry of Italian culture, politics, and architecture. This chapter will take you through the history of Montepulciano and will highlight key moments that shaped the town into the charming destination it is today.

The roots of Montepulciano can be found in the Etruscan civilization, which inhabited the region over two millennia ago. The Etruscans, known for their advanced agricultural and artistic practices, laid the groundwork for the fertile landscapes that define Montepulciano. As the Roman Empire expanded, the area became a crucial agricultural center, contributing wine and agricultural products to the Roman economy.

During the medieval period, Montepulciano began to take shape as a fortified settlement. Its strategic location on a hill provided a natural defense, and the town's defensive walls and towers were constructed to withstand external threats. This period also saw the rise of noble families like the Poliziani, who played a pivotal role in shaping the town's political and economic landscape.

By the 14th century, Montepulciano had established itself as a thriving medieval commune. The town's wealth grew through trade, agriculture, and the production of its renowned wine, Vino Nobile di Montepulciano. This red wine, crafted from the Sangiovese grape variety, became a symbol

View from Montepulciano facing west

of the region's viticultural excellence and added to Montepulciano's prestige.

During the Renaissance, Montepulciano experienced a cultural and artistic flourishing. The Poliziani family, in particular, commissioned renowned architects to design palaces and churches, leaving behind a legacy of impressive Renaissance architecture. The Palazzo Comunale, with its elegant facade and tower, stands as a testament to this period of prosperity.

However, the Renaissance also brought political instability to Italy, and Montepulciano was not immune. The town found itself caught in the crossfire of conflicts between rival city-states, including Florence and Siena. The power struggles of the time left a mark on Montepulciano, as various factions vied for control.

The 16th century brought about a significant transformation in Montepulciano with the arrival of the architect Antonio da Sangallo the Elder. His influence is evident in the redesign of the Piazza Grande, the town's main square, and the construction of the stunning San Biagio Church just outside the city walls. The church, with its impressive dome and harmonious proportions, is a masterpiece of Renaissance architecture.

Montepulciano continued to thrive culturally and economically throughout the following centuries, even as Italy underwent various political changes. The town's resilience and commitment to preserving its artistic and architectural heritage helped it weather the storms of history.

In the 19th century, Montepulciano, like the rest of Italy, experienced the unification process known as the Risorgimento. The town became part of the Kingdom of Italy in 1861, marking the end of the era of independent city-states. This period also brought about social and economic changes, challenging the traditional way of life in Montepulciano.

In the 20th century, Montepulciano faced the challenges of modernization while striving to maintain its cultural identity. The town adapted to the demands of the contemporary world, embracing tourism and preserving its historic charm. Visitors flocked to Montepulciano not only for its historical significance but also for its scenic beauty, delicious cuisine, and, of course, its world-renowned wines.

Montepulciano Real Estate Market

The real estate market in Montepulciano has really taken off the last 10 years. Driven by it's limited supply both within the historic center and in the countryside, property prices have risen steadily but have seen an acceleration in the last four years. With the popularity of the area for tourism increasing yearly, the demand for high quality rentals within the historic district has also increased. It is now very difficult to find a good quality rental for under €250,000. Outside the historic walls you can still find apartments at almost any price point, however they may not be very rentable for the tourist trade.

The driving force behind the steady rise in real estate prices here is the yearly growth in the high end tourist traffic visiting the city. The more these well heeled tourists visit the city, the higher the rates for apartments and homes that could service them will go.
The Montepulciano area is well known for wines and land designated for the production of grapes that are certified

Grapevines near Montepulciano

Nobile di Montepulciano sell for about €150,000 per hectare. That is about US$75,000 per U.S. Acre.

In addition to that is the fact that there is no new building allowed for homes in the countryside in much of the greater Southern Tuscany area.

The only way to get the rights to build a large new home is to "rebuild" a former farmhouse that is a ruin. But even the rebuild will be restricted to having the same footprint as the original house and also the same look as much as that can be accomplished. So when you are buying the ruins of an old farmhouse, you are really buying the rights to build a house more or less to your liking on the inside, but staying true to the original home on the outside. The cost for rebuilding a total ruin is about €2,000/MQ or about $220/sq ft. Then you have to add the cost of the old farmhouse and

San Biago, Montepulciano, Tuscany

land, which even in a completely uninhabitable state could still be $500,000-$1,000,000 or more. So your total cost for rebuilding a farmhouse including original farmhouse and the reconstruction of it can be well over $1,000,000 even for a smaller home.

It is very important that you research your plans to rebuild an old farmhouse. There are many restrictions and the process can take 12-18 months just for approval of plans and permitting. Talk to your real estate agent and find yourself a great architect if you are planning to go this route. Taking an old farmhouse and making it new again can be a fun and rewarding experience. But it can also be a money pit if not handled correctly and with the professional help that you will need.

Siena, Tuscany

Population: 53,000 (2022)
Elevation: 322 m (1,056 ft)

Piazza del Campo, Siena, Tuscany

    Siena has a history dating back many 1000's of years in the highlands of what is now Tuscany. Even the earliest inhabitants of the area recognized the importance of the position of this hilltop town. In the shadowy corridors of antiquity, the Etruscans, a civilization of enigmatic origin, cast their gaze upon the rolling hills that cradle Siena. They, with a mastery of the arts and an insatiable curiosity, shaped the land and left an indelible mark upon its destiny. Though the whispers of their language may have faded with the winds of time, the echoes of their existence resonate in the very earth of Siena.

As the ages unfolded, the Roman legions, like titans of old, traversed the Italian landscape, subsuming Etruscan realms into their mighty empire. Siena, once a humble Etruscan settlement, bowed to the imperial yoke, yet the essence of its spirit endured. The fall of Rome ushered in an era of transformation, a crucible from which medieval Siena emerged, phoenix-like, as a commune of fervent individuality.

Piazza del Campo, Siena, Tuscany

The heart of Siena, the Piazza del Campo, a grand amphitheater of life, became the canvas upon which the city painted its narrative. A tapestry woven with the threads of communal celebrations and civic pride, the Piazza bore witness to the dawn of Siena's artistic identity. Amidst its cobblestone expanse, a vibrant marketplace for ideas and creativity burgeoned, fostering a unique cultural spirit.

The ecclesiastical realm, embodied in the resplendent Duomo di Siena, became the sanctum where the divine and artistic converged. The cathedral, a testament to faith and architectural prowess, housed treasures of unparalleled artistic magnificence. Duccio di Buoninsegna, a maestro of his time, bestowed upon the Duomo the Maestà, a masterpiece that transcended the earthly realm with its luminous hues and ethereal grace.

The Quattrocento, a golden age of artistic expression, enveloped Siena in a Renaissance embrace. The city, though overshadowed by the burgeoning brilliance of Florence, stood as a sanctuary for a distinct artistic tradition – the Sienese School. Visionaries like Giovanni di Paolo and Matteo di Giovanni graced the canvas with their virtuosity, infusing Siena's art with a unique vibrancy.

The *Allegory of Good and Bad Government*, a fresco by Ambrogio Lorenzetti adorning the Palazzo Pubblico, embodied the ideals of civic responsibility and governance. Siena, a republic of enlightened minds, sought to translate these ideals into the very fabric of its societal structure.

As the Renaissance waned, the spirit of Siena persisted, an indomitable flame lighting the path through the annals of time. The chiaroscuro of the city's history painted by luminaries like Bernardino di Betto, known as Pinturicchio, showcased the enduring legacy of artistic brilliance.

Siena Cathedral (1263).   Siena, Italy

In the symphony of Siena's cultural heritage, art and identity danced in harmonious celebration. The Tuscan landscape, with its rolling hills and vineyards, mirrored the palette of Sienese art – a tapestry of warm ochres, rich siennas, and deep umbers. The people of Siena, inheritors of an illustrious past, embraced their cultural heritage with a passion that transcended the epochs.

The history of Siena unfolds as a tale of Etruscan whispers, medieval fortitude, and Renaissance grandness. The city, adorned with the treasures of its artistic legacy, stands as a testament to the enduring power of culture. Siena, a jewel in the crown of Italia, beckons to those who seek to traverse the corridors of time and immerse themselves in the timeless embrace of its art and heritage.

Siena Real Estate Market

Like many towns in Italy, prices in Siena's real estate market are influenced heavily by the tourist trade. With well over 1 million tourists each year, Siena is one of the most popular destinations in Tuscany. Apartments in the historic district demand a premium because of the rental demands of these tourists.

For example, a 2 bedroom 2 bath apartment in Siena will probably cost around €350,000 minimum. An apartment with an outside terrace or even better, a view of the Piazza del Campo will be much more. Even during the economic crisis of 2008-2010, there was very little downward pressure on the pricing in Siena. Part of the reason is many of the properties are still owned by families who have controlled them for years. Therefore there is little pressure to sell during temporary downturns as there is usually no outstanding loans on the apartments.

Like many other towns in Italy, once you are outside the historic district, the prices for apartments and homes drops dramatically. Siena is surrounded by many other smaller towns and villages that will allow you to come into the city proper within 10 minutes or less, but will lower your cost of housing versus the city center by more than 50%.

Siena is one of the towns in Italy where the rental market stays strong almost all year long, with perhaps a slight slow down in late January and February. But with smart marketing and price incentives, you can probably keep the apartments rented then as well.

Perugia, Umbria

**Population: 161,000 (2022)
Elevation: 493 m (1,617 ft)**

Amidst the undulating landscapes of Italia, where the verdant hills hold secrets whispered through the ages, the ancient city of Perugia stands as a testament to the rich tapestry of Italian history. From its Etruscan origins to the medieval splendors and beyond, Perugia's narrative unfolds like a captivating epic.

Perugia, Umbria

Scalinata Steps, Perugia, Umbria

In the shadows of antiquity, the Etruscans, masters of mystery and artistry, laid the foundations of what would later become Perugia. Their presence, like elusive phantoms in the historical records, permeated the land, leaving behind enigmatic tombs and artifacts that hinted at their once-thriving civilization. The Etruscans, with their advanced knowledge and vibrant culture, imbued the soil of Perugia with a legacy that lingered through the corridors of time.

With the rise of the Roman Empire, Perugia, like many Etruscan settlements, fell under the imperial sway. The sturdy stones of Roman construction bore witness to the city's integration into the vast tapestry of Roman dominion.

The triumphal arches and ancient amphitheaters, fragments of which endure, narrate the tales of Perugia's Roman past.

As the Roman era waned, the tumultuous waves of history ushered in the medieval epoch, and Perugia emerged as a sovereign commune of formidable stature. The city, perched atop a hill with commanding views of the surrounding Umbrian landscape, became a bastion of independence. The resolute Perugini defended their freedom fiercely, etching their mark on the annals of Italian medieval history.

The Palazzo dei Priori, a formidable fortress-like structure that graces the heart of Perugia, stands as a testament to the city's medieval prominence. Within its walls, the echoes of councils and deliberations resound, reflecting the civic pride and autonomy of the Perugian people. The Fontana Maggiore, a monumental fountain adorned with intricate sculptures, further exemplifies the city's commitment to artistic expression even in the midst of political life.

Perugia's artistic legacy burgeoned during the Renaissance, as the city embraced the transformative currents of the time. The illustrious artist Pietro Vannucci, better known as Perugino, emerged as a luminary in the artistic firmament. His works, such as the frescoes in the Collegio del Cambio, exemplify the grace and serenity characteristic of the Umbrian school of painting.

However, Perugia's history was not without tumult. The city found itself entangled in the complex web of Italian city-states and the shifting allegiances of the time. The struggle for dominance and control played out in the conflicts between Perugia and neighboring cities, most notably the protracted wars with Assisi and the machinations of the Papal States.

Perugia, Umbria

The Renaissance spirit that permeated Perugia also found expression in the architectural marvel of the Rocca Paolina, a fortress commissioned by Pope Paul III. Beneath its imposing structure lies the medieval heart of Perugia, a subterranean city encapsulating the layers of history that the city had witnessed.

Perugia, with its rich cultural tapestry, continued to flourish into the modern era. The University of Perugia, founded in the 13th century, evolved into a center of learning and intellectual exchange. The city's commitment to education and culture echoed through the centuries, fostering an environment that celebrated both tradition and innovation.

In conclusion, Perugia's history unfolds as a captivating saga, where the whispers of the Etruscans linger, the echoes of Roman grandeur resonate, and the medieval and Renaissance chapters narrate tales of resilience and artistic brilliance. This ancient city, with its hilltop perch and labyrinthine streets, invites the discerning traveler to traverse the corridors of time and immerse themselves in the multifaceted beauty of Perugia's past.

Perugia Real Estate Market

Perugia is located about 2 hours from both Rome and Florence. It's location near to Assisi, Todi, Spello and Spoleto also makes it a famous destination for tourists. While the city is much more affordable than Florence or Lucca, it is still a good market to own apartments in. If you are looking for a town with all services but not with the overwhelming tourist flows of Florence and Rome, then Perugia might be your type of living environment.

The real estate market in most towns is so variable that trying in this format to pin down exact pricing is virtually impossible. Suffices to say that the real estate market in Perugia is somewhat less expensive than in areas like Florence or Venice or Rome. You should be able to find a very nicely appointed three-bedroom home outside of the city center for between €200-€300,000 for a medium size home. Apartments outside the city center can be bought for starting under €100,000 depending on the quality and the condition. Perugia is a very beautiful city to come and visit and during the off-season which is anything other than summer. You should be able to find a medium term rental that won't break your budget. Come and spend one month in the town and really get to know the people and the area.

TODI, UMBRIA

Population: 16,000 (2023)
Elevation: 410 m (1345 ft)

Todi, Italy

Todi is a picturesque town nestled in the heart of Umbria, and it boasts a rich history that dates back thousands of years. With its medieval charm, ancient roots, and stunning landscapes, Todi has become a destination that captivates visitors seeking a glimpse into the past.

The origins of Todi can be traced to the ancient Etruscan civilization, which thrived in central Italy from the 8th to the 3rd century BCE. The Etruscans, known for their advanced culture and artistry, left a significant imprint on the region, and Todi stands as a testament to their influence. The town's strategic location on a hill provided natural defenses, and its proximity to the Tiber River facilitated trade and communication with neighboring regions.

Cathedral, Lodi, Italy

As the Roman Republic expanded its dominion, Todi came under Roman control in the 3rd century BCE. The Romans, recognizing the strategic importance of the town, fortified and developed it further. The remnants of Roman walls, amphitheaters, and temples still bear witness to this era, offering a glimpse into Todi's role as a flourishing Roman municipality.

With the fall of the Roman Empire in the 5th century, Todi, like many other Italian towns, experienced a period of decline. However, the town managed to endure through the tumultuous centuries that followed, finding itself under the rule of various medieval powers, including the Byzantines and Lombards. In the 11th century, Todi gained newfound prominence when it became a free commune, asserting its independence and establishing a self-governing system.

The medieval period marked a golden age for Todi, as the town flourished culturally and economically. Magnificent churches, palaces, and civic buildings adorned the landscape, reflecting the prosperity of the community. Todi's iconic cathedral, dedicated to Santa Maria Annunziata, stands as a prime example of the architectural grandeur of this era, with its intricate facade and stunning interior.

The Renaissance brought further enhancements to Todi's architectural and artistic legacy. The town became a hub for intellectual and artistic pursuits, attracting renowned painters, sculptors, and architects. The Piazza del Popolo, Todi's main square, is a testament to the Renaissance influence, featuring the

Hill View, Todi, Italy

Palazzo dei Priori, a magnificent palace adorned with elegant arches and a distinctive clock tower.

During the 16th century, Todi experienced a period of political and social upheaval as various external forces sought control. The town oscillated between papal rule and local governance, facing challenges such as the Sack of Todi in 1527, a violent episode during the Italian War of 1521-1526. Despite these challenges, Todi managed to retain its cultural vibrancy and architectural splendor.

Historic Center, Todi

The subsequent centuries witnessed Todi adapting to changing political landscapes and economic dynamics. The town's strategic importance waned, but its historical charm endured. In the 20th century, Todi, like many Italian towns, faced the challenges of modernization while striving to preserve its cultural heritage. Efforts were made to safeguard historic sites, and the town became a magnet for those seeking a retreat to the tranquility of its medieval surroundings.

Today visitors can wander through its narrow cobblestone streets, marvel at its medieval architecture, and soak in the panoramic views of the surrounding

Umbrian countryside. Todi's annual events, such as the Todi Festival and the Todi Arte Festival, celebrate its cultural richness, ensuring that the town remains a dynamic hub of art, history, and tradition.

Todi Real Estate Market

The real estate market in Todd is solid due to it's popularity with retirees and expats. Less than 2 hours from Rome's Fiumicino airport and on a major highway and rail line makes it also very attractive. While Todi is a hilltop village of about 16,000 people, the surrounding area encompasses many other towns and villages that bring the total population to a much higher level.

There are hospitals in the immediate area to service the town and a regional hospital is only 25 minutes away in Perugia. Of course all services from large supermarkets, large box stores like hardware, clothing shops and home goods can be found within a 15 minute drive

Todi receives its fair share of tourists each year. It is not a major tourist town on the level of Florence or Lucca, but it's close proximity to Rome makes it a great trip for a short term rental apartment to operate in. You can find very nice apartments in Todi for under €200,000 that would be of the quality that would be expected on the nightly rental market like VRBO or AirBnB.

Inside the historic center it will be difficult to find a independent house, but you can find many nice apartments. Once you are outside the historic center and in the area down below you will find more modern homes built in the 1960-70's. These homes will be at a lower price per square meter than the same quality of dwellings in the historic center. There is so much variation in the pricing for homes here that it is not possible to give an exact figure on the costs, other than to say it is much cheaper in Todi then in other larger medieval and renaissance towns that draw in millions of tourists a year.

ORVIETO, UMBRIA

Population: 19,400 (2023)
Elevation: 325 m (1066 ft)

Orvieto, Umbria

Orvieto, a picturesque ton perched on a volcanic plateau in the Umbria region of Italy, boasts a rich and storied history that spans thousands of years. Its strategic location, commanding views, and architectural wonders make it a captivating destination for history enthusiasts and travelers alike.

The origins of Orvieto can be traced back to the Etruscans, an ancient civilization that thrived in central Italy before the rise of Rome. The Etruscans settled in the area around the 9th century BCE, attracted by the fertile volcanic soil and defensible terrain. Orvieto, known as Velzna in Etruscan times, became a flourishing center for trade and commerce. The Etruscans were skilled in hydraulic engineering, and they carved intricate tunnels and wells into the soft volcanic rock, creating an elaborate network to provide water to the city.

As the Roman Republic expanded its influence in the 3rd

Country Side Near Orvieto, Umbria

century BCE, Orvieto fell under Roman control. The Romans recognized the strategic significance of the city and further developed its infrastructure, including the construction of a temple dedicated to the god Jupiter. Orvieto continued to thrive under Roman rule, becoming an essential stop on the road connecting Rome to the northern regions of Italy.

With the decline of the Roman Empire, Orvieto experienced a period of instability and change. The city faced invasions from various Germanic tribes, including the Visigoths and Ostrogoths. However, it managed to maintain a degree of autonomy and stability, thanks in part to its strategic location atop a volcanic plateau, which provided a natural defensive barrier.

In the Middle Ages, Orvieto emerged as a powerful and independent city-state. The city's prosperity was fueled by its agricultural wealth, flourishing trade, and the production of high-quality ceramics. Orvieto's distinctive pottery, known as "Orvietano," became renowned for its intricate designs and vibrant colors, and it played a significant role in the city's economic success.

One of the most iconic landmarks of Orvieto, the Cathedral of Santa Maria Assunta, began construction in 1290 and took several centuries to complete. The cathedral is a masterpiece of Italian Gothic architecture, featuring a façade adorned with stunning mosaics, sculptures, and bas-reliefs. The interior houses notable works of art, including Luca Signorelli's frescoes in the San Brizio Chapel, depicting scenes from the Last Judgment.

During the 14th century, Orvieto faced internal strife and external threats. The city-state was caught in the power struggles between the Guelphs and Ghibellines, two factions vying for control in medieval Italy. Additionally, Orvieto found itself in conflict with other nearby city-states, including Perugia and Siena. Despite these challenges, the city managed to maintain its independence and continued to be a cultural and economic hub.
Orvieto's golden age came to an end in the 16th century when it fell under the dominion of the Papal States. The popes, recognizing the strategic importance of the city,

fortified it further and used it as a summer residence. The city's fortunes declined, but its historical and artistic significance endured. The Renaissance period left its mark on Orvieto, with the construction of elegant palaces, churches, and public buildings.

In the 19th century, Orvieto played a role in the unification of Italy. As the various Italian states sought to unify under a single flag, Orvieto, like many other regions, experienced political and social changes. The city became part of the Kingdom of Italy in 1860, marking a new chapter in its history.

In the modern era, Orvieto has embraced its heritage and become a popular tourist destination. Visitors are drawn to its well-preserved medieval architecture, charming streets, and the breathtaking views from the city's elevated position. The city's underground tunnels and caves, remnants of its Etruscan past, also attract curious travelers.

Orvieto's history is a testament to the resilience of a city that has weathered centuries of change and conflict. From its Etruscan roots to its medieval glory and subsequent challenges, Orvieto stands as a living testament to Italy's rich cultural and historical tapestry. Today, as visitors wander through its cobbled streets and marvel at its architectural wonders, they are reminded of the enduring legacy of this remarkable Italian city.

Orvieto Real Estate Market

Orvieto is an easy 90 minute trip from Rome by car or in the train. Since it is one of the largest and most convenient medieval and renaissance towns to visit outside of Rome, it has become very popular for short term rentals. This of course has driven up the price of rental properties within the historic walls. But you will still find that apartments for sale that would be appropriate for the short term rental business are more reasonable compared to cities like Florence or Siena.

Orvieto, Italy

Outside the historic center there are many villas for sale, but the pricing can be rather high. Expect to spend well over €400.000 for an updated villa with a little land (less than 1 hectare). Home prices can easily top €1M or more in the area. Of course there are many more reasonably priced homes close to the town, but in the flat areas. You can expect to be able to find a home for €200-350,000. Apartments not in the historic district can start as low as €75,000 for something in good condition but needing updating. Usually they will need some sort of DIY updating or light remodelling like new bathrooms or kitchens.

It is relatively easy to find good quality craftsman in almost all areas of Italy. Orvietto is one of these places…. Your real estate agent should be able to put you in contact with any type of contractor that you may need. Likewise, a good real estate agent will know people that are available to do property rentals should you decide to put a good prospect for nightly rentals onto the tourist market.

ROME

Population: 2,748,109 (2023)
Greater Metro Area: 2,870,000 (2023)
Elevation: 21 m (69 ft)

Coliseum, Rome Italy

Rome, a city with a rich and storied history, has been a symbol of power, civilization, and cultural achievement for over two millennia. From its legendary foundation in the 8th century BC to the present day, Rome has witnessed the rise and fall of empires, the spread of Christianity, and the evolution of political and social structures. This comprehensive history of Rome will cover key events and periods, including the Roman Republic, the Roman Empire, the Middle Ages, the Renaissance, and modern times.

Pantheon, Rome, Italy

**Founding and Early Republic
(8th - 5th centuries BC)**

Legend has it that Rome was founded in 753 BC by Romulus and Remus, twin brothers raised by a she-wolf. The early Romans were primarily farmers and shepherds, organizing themselves into a monarchy. However, in 509 BC, the Roman Republic was established, marking the beginning of a new political era. The republic was characterized by a system of checks and balances, with power distributed among elected officials, known as senators and consuls.

Punic Wars and Expansion
(3rd - 2nd centuries BC)

During the 3rd and 2nd centuries BC, Rome engaged in a series of conflicts with Carthage known as the Punic Wars. The most famous of these was the Second Punic War (218-201 BC), where Rome faced the brilliant Carthaginian general Hannibal. Despite initial setbacks, Rome emerged victorious, gaining control of territories in the Mediterranean and solidifying its status as a major power.

Julius Caesar and the End of the Republic
(1st century BC)

As the Roman Republic expanded, internal strife and power struggles intensified. In 49 BC, Julius Caesar, a military general, crossed the Rubicon River, defying the Senate's order to disband his army. This act triggered a civil war between Caesar and his rival, Pompey. In 44 BC, Julius Caesar was assassinated, leading to further political chaos. Eventually, Caesar's adopted heir, Octavian (later known as Augustus), emerged victorious, marking the end of the Roman Republic and the beginning of the Roman Empire.

Pax Romana and the Height of the Empire
(1st - 2nd centuries AD)

Under Augustus, the Roman Empire experienced a period of relative peace known as the Pax Romana (27 BC - 180 AD). During this time, the empire expanded its borders, reaching its greatest territorial extent under Emperor Trajan. Rome became a hub of culture, trade, and innovation, with impressive architectural feats such as the Colosseum and the Pantheon.

Decline and Fall of the Western Roman Empire
(3rd - 5th centuries AD)

Despite its prosperity, the Roman Empire faced internal and external challenges in the 3rd century AD. Economic troubles, military defeats, and political instability contributed to the decline of the Western Roman Empire. In 476 AD, the last Roman emperor, Romulus Augustulus, was overthrown by the Germanic chieftain Odoacer, marking the traditional date for the fall of the Western Roman Empire.

Byzantine Empire and the Eastern Roman Empire
(4th - 15th centuries AD)

While the Western Roman Empire crumbled, the Eastern Roman Empire, later known as the Byzantine Empire, continued to thrive. Centered in Constantinople (modern-day Istanbul), the Byzantine Empire preserved Roman traditions and culture for nearly a millennium. It withstood various threats, including invasions by the Visigoths, Vandals, and later the Ottoman Turks, until Constantinople fell in 1453, marking the end of the Byzantine Empire.

Medieval Rome and the Papal States
(5th - 15th centuries AD)

In the absence of a centralized Roman authority, the city of Rome entered a period of decline and fragmentation during the early Middle Ages. The Papal States emerged as a significant political entity, with the pope serving as both a spiritual and temporal leader. Rome became a focal point of medieval Christianity, hosting pilgrims and acting as a center for religious power.

Churches, Rome, Italy

**Renaissance and the Rebirth of Rome
(14th - 17th centuries)**

The Renaissance brought a revival of interest in classical Roman art, literature, and philosophy. Rome experienced a cultural reawakening, with artists like Michelangelo, Raphael, and Leonardo da Vinci contributing to the city's architectural and artistic splendor. The construction of St. Peter's Basilica, the Sistine Chapel, and other iconic structures transformed Rome into a center of artistic and intellectual innovation.

***Baroque Rome and Papal Dominance
(17th - 18th centuries)***

The Baroque period in the 17th and 18th centuries left an indelible mark on Rome's architecture and urban planning. Popes such as Urban VIII and Innocent X commissioned grand projects like the Trevi Fountain and the Spanish Steps. Rome became a symbol of Catholic Counter-Reformation, reaffirming its position as the heart of the Catholic Church.

Napoleonic Era and the Roman Republic (18th - 19th centuries)

Napoleon Bonaparte's conquest of Italy in the late 18th century led to the establishment of the Roman Republic in 1798, a short-lived experiment in republicanism. However, the Napoleonic era also saw the rise of nationalism and the eventual resurgence of the Papal States under the Congress of Vienna in 1815.

Italian Unification and the Capture of Rome (19th century)

The 19th century witnessed the unification of Italy, culminating in 1871 when Rome became the capital of the newly unified Italian state. The Papal States were incorporated into the Kingdom of Italy, and Rome was declared the capital by King Victor Emmanuel II. This event marked the end of the temporal power of the papacy.

World Wars and Mussolini's Rome (20th century)

Rome played a significant role in both World War I and World War II. Italy, initially allied with Germany and Austria-Hungary, switched sides in World War I and faced economic hardships during the interwar period. In the 1920s, Benito Mussolini's fascist government came to power, bringing a period of authoritarian rule. Rome underwent extensive urban development projects, including the construction of the Via dei Fori Imperiali.

Castel Sant'Angelo, Rome, Italy

Post-War Rome and the European Union (20th - 21st centuries)

After World War II, Italy underwent a period of reconstruction, and Rome emerged as a cultural and diplomatic hub. In 1957, Rome hosted the signing of the Treaty of Rome, which established the European Economic Community (EEC), a precursor to the European Union. The city continued to grow as a global center for art, culture, and diplomacy in the latter half of the 20th century and into the 21st century.

The legacy of Rome endures in its architectural marvels, artistic treasures, and contributions to law, governance, and culture. As a modern capital, Rome continues to be a living testament to its enduring past while adapting to the challenges and opportunities of the present.

Rome Real Estate Market

The real estate market in Rome has been experiencing both challenges and opportunities in recent years. As a city with a rich history, stunning architecture, and a thriving cultural scene, Rome has always been a desirable location for real estate investment. However, various factors have contributed to fluctuations in the market, impacting pricing and statistics.

Door in Rome, Italy

One of the key elements affecting the real estate market in Rome is the economic climate. Italy, as a whole, has faced economic challenges, and these have inevitably influenced the housing market in the capital city. The global economic downturn, compounded by domestic economic issues, has led to a degree of uncertainty among investors and potential buyers. Consequently, the market has seen shifts in pricing dynamics.

Caption

As of the latest available data, Rome's real estate market has displayed a trend of moderate growth, with prices maintaining relative stability. The average price per square meter in prime areas of the city, such as the historic center, has seen a modest increase. However, it's essential to note that these figures can vary significantly depending on the specific neighborhood, property type, and condition.

The demand for real estate in Rome remains robust, driven by both domestic and international interest. Foreign investors, attracted by the city's historical significance and cultural appeal, continue to play a significant role in the market. Additionally, local buyers seek properties for both residential and investment purposes, contributing to the overall demand.
The rental market in Rome also plays a crucial role in the

Boat on Tiber River - Rome, Italy

real estate landscape. The city's popularity as a tourist destination has led to a thriving short-term rental market. Many property owners choose to capitalize on the tourism industry by renting their properties to visitors.

Rome is the pinnacle of the Italian real estate market. Apartment prices within the city center of Rome are astronomical compared to the rest of the country, with the exception of perhaps Florence and Venice. A good quality and well located two bedroom/two bath apartment in the Rome city center can easily top €1 million. The reason for this is because of the huge influx of tourists that Rome receives every year.

It's estimated by the Vatican and the Rome Tourism Board that in the year 2025 when the Catholic Church is celebrating its Jubilee, Italy as a whole will receive 55 million tourists in addition to the normal yearly influx (this is over the course of the entire year that the Jubilee runs). The majority of these tourists will find their way to Rome. It is said that in Rome, good quality rental apartments can be rented virtually every single day of the year. Rental rates for apartments to the tourist trade are quite high and the return on investment (ROI) for them can be very good. The key is in the buying of the apartment and the execution of the renting it out.

NAPLES, CAMPANIA

Population: 909,048 (2023)
Greater Metro Area: 3,115,000 (2023)
Elevation: 100 m (327 ft)

Mount Vesuvius, Naples, Italy

Naples, the vibrant and historic city located in southern Italy, has a rich and diverse history that spans thousands of years. Its origins can be traced back to the ancient Greeks, who established the city as a colony around the 8th century BC. Originally known as Parthenope, the settlement thrived due to its strategic location on the Gulf of Naples and its fertile surroundings.

In the 6th century BC, Naples was conquered by the Etruscans and later by the Samnites, an Italic people. The city underwent a series of transformations and name changes during this period. Eventually, the Romans took control of Naples in the 4th century BC, integrating it into the growing Roman Republic. Under Roman rule, Naples flourished as a key commercial and cultural center. The

Naples, Italy

Romans constructed important infrastructure such as aqueducts, theaters, and temples, leaving a lasting imprint on the city's landscape.

After the fall of the Roman Empire, Naples went through a turbulent period of invasions and conquests by various Germanic tribes, including the Ostrogoths and the Lombards. However, it was the Byzantines who ultimately regained control in the 6th century AD. Naples became a part of the Byzantine Duchy of Naples, marking a period of relative stability.

The Norman Conquest in the 11th century brought significant changes to Naples. The Normans, led by Robert Guiscard, captured the city and established the Kingdom of Sicily, which included Naples. The subsequent Swabian and Angevin rulers contributed to the city's cultural and architectural development. During this time, Naples experienced a flourishing period of art and scholarship, exemplified by the construction of the Castel Nuovo and the creation of the University of Naples.

In the 15th century, Naples faced a new wave of challenges with the arrival of the Aragonese dynasty. The city became embroiled in conflicts, including the War of the Sicilian Vespers, which resulted in the Spanish Crown taking control of Naples in 1504. The Spanish Habsburgs ruled Naples for several centuries, leaving an enduring impact on the city's architecture and culture.

The 17th century brought both prosperity and adversity to Naples. The city experienced a period of economic growth and artistic flourishing known as the Baroque Naples. Notable landmarks, such as the Royal Palace of Naples and the Church of Gesù Nuovo, were built during this time. However, Naples also faced devastating challenges, including outbreaks of the bubonic plague and a series of earthquakes that caused widespread destruction.

Street in Naples, Italy

In the late 18th century, Naples played a pivotal role in the Italian unification movement. The city became a hotbed of revolutionary activity, leading to the establishment of the Parthenopean Republic in 1799. However, the short-lived republic was crushed by the Bourbon monarchy and their supporters. Naples subsequently became a part of the Kingdom of Two Sicilies, ruled by the Bourbon dynasty.

The 19th century witnessed significant political and social changes in Naples. Giuseppe Garibaldi, a key figure in the unification of Italy, led the Expedition of the Thousand, a military campaign that resulted in the annexation of Naples to the Kingdom of Italy in 1860. Naples became an integral part of the newly unified Italy, but the transition was not without challenges. The city struggled with issues such as poverty and political unrest.

In the 20th century, Naples faced the impact of World War II, with the city suffering extensive damage during bombings. Despite the destruction, Naples quickly recovered and underwent a process of post-war reconstruction. In the latter half of the century, the city experienced economic growth and became a popular tourist destination, attracting visitors with its rich history, vibrant culture, and culinary delights. Today, Naples stands as a testament to its storied past, with

Naples, Italy

a blend of ancient ruins, medieval structures, and modern developments. The city's historical significance, coupled with its unique charm, continues to attract people from around the world, making Naples a captivating destination that reflects the enduring spirit of its inhabitants and the diverse cultures that have shaped its history.

Naples Real Estate Market

Naples, located in the southern part of Italy, is renowned for its rich history, cultural heritage, and stunning landscapes. The real estate market in Naples reflects a unique blend of historical charm and modern aspirations. This detailed analysis aims to provide insights into the current state of the real estate market in Naples, exploring key trends, factors influencing the market, and future prospects.

Market Overview

The real estate market in Naples is characterized by a diverse range of properties, from historic apartments in the city center to luxurious villas along the Amalfi Coast. Naples has witnessed a steady increase in property values over the past decade, driven by factors such as improved infrastructure, growing tourism, and a renewed interest in Italian real estate from both domestic and international investors.

Trends and Influencing Factors

1. Cultural and Historical Appeal
   Naples' historical significance and cultural attractions contribute significantly to the real estate market. Old town districts, like Spaccanapoli, offer unique properties with

Naples, Italy

historic charm, attracting buyers seeking a blend of tradition and modern living.

2. Tourism Impact

Naples is a major tourist destination, and this has a dual impact on the real estate market. On one hand, short-term rentals, especially in the city center, are lucrative for property owners. On the other hand, increased tourism can drive demand for properties as investors look to capitalize on the potential rental income.

3. Infrastructure Development

Ongoing infrastructure projects, including the Naples Metro expansion and improvements to transportation networks, enhance connectivity and accessibility. Improved infrastructure often leads to increased property values, especially in areas benefiting from these developments.

4. Foreign Investment
Naples has become an attractive destination for foreign investors seeking real estate opportunities in Italy. The appeal lies not only in the historical and cultural richness but also in the potential for high returns on investment, particularly in the luxury property segment.

5. Market Stability and Economic Factors
Italy's economic stability, political landscape, and global economic conditions play a crucial role in shaping the real estate market. Economic uncertainties can impact buyer confidence and influence investment decisions.

Castel Nuovo, Naples, Italy

Current Market Dynamics

As of the latest data, the Naples real estate market is experiencing a stable yet dynamic phase. The demand for properties in prime locations remains high, driving price appreciation in sought-after neighborhoods. Luxury properties, especially those with panoramic views of the Bay of Naples, are in high demand, attracting affluent buyers.

The city center, with its historic architecture and cultural landmarks, continues to be a focal point for real estate activity. The revitalization of neglected areas has opened up opportunities for developers and investors to transform older properties into modern residences, contributing to the overall gentrification of certain neighborhoods.

Challenges and Risks
While the Naples real estate market presents promising opportunities, it is not without challenges. Regulatory changes, fluctuating market conditions, and potential oversupply in certain segments are risks that investors and developers need to navigate. Additionally, concerns about the environmental impact, particularly in coastal areas, pose challenges for sustainable development.

Future Prospects

The outlook for the Naples real estate market appears positive, driven by factors such as continued tourism growth, infrastructure development, and the city's enduring cultural appeal. However, stakeholders must remain vigilant in adapting to changing market dynamics and proactively addressing challenges to ensure long-term sustainability.

The real estate market in Naples, Italy, stands at the intersection of history, culture, and modernity. The city's

unique charm, coupled with strategic investments and infrastructure development, positions Naples as an attractive destination for both domestic and international real estate investors. As the market evolves, stakeholders must embrace innovation and sustainable practices to harness the full potential of this dynamic real estate landscape..
.

LECCE, PUGLIA

Population: 95,000 (2022)
Elevation: 49 m (161 ft)

Ostuni, Near Lecce, Puglia

Lecce, situated in the southern region of Italy's Apulia, or Puglia, is a city with a rich history dating back thousands of years. The origins of Lecce are rooted in ancient times, with evidence of human settlement in the area during the Bronze Age. However, it was under the Roman Empire that Lecce truly began to flourish.

During the Roman period, Lecce gained prominence as a strategic hub due to its location on the crossroads of important trade routes. The city, known as Lupiae in Roman times, became a thriving center for commerce, culture, and governance. The Romans left a lasting mark on Lecce, evident in the well-preserved Roman amphitheater that stands as a testament to the city's ancient past.

As the Roman Empire declined, Lecce, like many other cities, faced a series of invasions and changes in rulership. The Byzantines took control of the region in the 6th century AD, bringing a period of stability and cultural influence. Lecce became an important center for Byzantine art and architecture, with notable examples such as the Basilica di Santa Maria della Croce, showcasing intricate mosaics and frescoes.

The Norman conquest in the 11th century brought Lecce under the rule of the Normans, who further contributed to the city's cultural and architectural heritage. The Normans erected fortifications and palaces, leaving behind structures that are still integral to Lecce's cityscape. Subsequent rulers, including the Swabians and the Angevins, continued to shape the city's identity through their influence on art and governance.

The Renaissance period marked another significant chapter in Lecce's history. During the 16th and 17th centuries, the city experienced a cultural and artistic renaissance, characterized by a flourishing of Baroque architecture. Lecce is particularly renowned for its unique style of Baroque known as "Lecce Baroque" or "Barocco Leccese." The Baroque period saw the construction of numerous ornate churches, palaces, and public buildings, adorned with intricate carvings and decorations. The Basilica di Santa

Croce and the Piazza del Duomo are prime examples of this distinctive architectural style.

In the 18th century, Lecce continued to thrive as a center of artistic expression and cultural innovation. The city's Baroque masterpieces attracted artists and architects, contributing to the grandeur of the urban landscape. The cultural richness of this period is also reflected in the craftsmanship of local artisans who excelled in creating intricate sculptures and carvings.

During the 19th century, Lecce, like the rest of Italy, witnessed the struggle for unification. The city played a role in the Risorgimento movement, which ultimately led to the formation of the Kingdom of Italy in 1861. Lecce became an integral part of the unified nation and experienced economic and social changes as a result.

In the 20th century, Lecce faced the challenges of modernization and urban development. The city preserved its historical and artistic treasures while adapting to the demands of a changing world. Today, Lecce stands as a vibrant blend of antiquity and modernity, attracting visitors with its well-preserved historic center, charming streets, and lively atmosphere.

Lecce's history visible in its streets, squares, and buildings. The city's ability to preserve its ancient roots while embracing cultural and artistic evolution has earned it a place as one of Italy's treasures, inviting travelers to explore its rich history and experience the beauty of Lecce Baroque.

Lecce Real Estate Market

Lecce's real estate market is characterized by a unique blend of historical properties, vibrant city life, and proximity to the picturesque Salento Peninsula. The city's architectural splendor, with its intricately carved Baroque facades, contributes to the overall appeal for those seeking a harmonious combination of tradition and modern living.

Trends and Influencing Factors

Historical Charm and Cultural Significance
Lecce's architectural treasures, such as the Basilica di Santa Croce and Piazza del Duomo, contribute significantly to the city's real estate charm. Properties within the historic center, characterized by narrow cobblestone streets and centuries-old buildings, often command a premium.

Tourism-Driven Opportunities
Lecce has become a popular tourist destination, attracting visitors with its unique architecture, gastronomy, and local crafts. This has led to a growing market for short-term rentals, particularly in the historic center, where tourists seek an authentic experience amid the Baroque wonders.

Renewed Interest in Italian Real Estate
The broader trend of increased interest in Italian real estate from both domestic and international investors has also influenced Lecce's market. The city's unique character and relatively lower property prices compared to other Italian cities make it an attractive option for those looking to invest in a distinctive cultural setting.

Local Economic Developments
Local economic growth and employment opportunities play a pivotal role in the real estate market. Lecce has seen

developments in industries such as renewable energy, technology, and tourism-related services, which contribute to increased demand for housing and potential investment opportunities.

Cultural Events and Festivals
Lecce hosts various cultural events and festivals throughout the year, drawing both locals and tourists. These events not only contribute to the city's vibrancy but also impact the real estate market by influencing property demand and rental trends during peak periods.

Current Market Dynamics
The real estate market in Lecce is experiencing positive dynamics. The demand for properties, especially within the historic center, remains robust. Baroque-style apartments and houses with original features are highly sought after, attracting both local and international buyers looking for unique and culturally rich residences.

The surge in tourism has led to a flourishing short-term rental market, with investors capitalizing on the city's appeal to vacationers. Additionally, there is a growing trend of property renovation, with investors and individuals alike seeking to restore and modernize historic buildings, contributing to the revitalization of certain neighborhoods.

Challenges and Risks

Despite the positive trends, challenges persist. Striking a balance between modernization and preserving the historical integrity of buildings is a delicate task. Regulatory hurdles and zoning restrictions may pose challenges for property development and renovation projects. Moreover, as with many tourist-centric areas, the seasonality of demand for short-term rentals may introduce income volatility for property owners.

Lecce, Puglia

Future Prospects

The future of Lecce's real estate market appears promising. Continued investments in local infrastructure, cultural preservation efforts, and the city's growing popularity as a tourist destination bode well for sustained market growth. However, stakeholders must remain vigilant to address challenges, such as urban planning and the need for sustainable development, to ensure the long-term success of the market.

Lecce's real estate market is full of historical charm, cultural richness, and modern aspirations. As the city continues to draw attention from investors and those seeking a unique living experience, strategic planning, and a delicate balance between preservation and development will be key to unlocking the full potential of Lecce's real estate landscape..

SICILY
Population: 4,983,000 (2018)

Greek Temple nighttime, Sicily, Italy

Sicily, the largest island in the Mediterranean Sea, has a history that spans thousands of years, marked by a tapestry of cultures, civilizations, and influences. From ancient times to the present day, Sicily's story is one of conquest, trade, cultural exchange, and resilience.

The earliest known inhabitants of Sicily were the indigenous Sicani, Elymians, and Sicels, who were gradually replaced by Phoenician and Greek colonizers around the 8th century BC. The Phoenicians established settlements on the western part of the island, while the Greeks founded colonies in the east, including Naxos and Syracuse. The city of Syracuse, in particular, would later become a powerful and influential center in Sicilian history.

Sicilian Hill Town

Sicily's strategic location made it a coveted prize for various powers in the ancient world. The Carthaginians, successors to the Phoenicians, clashed with the Greeks over control of the island during the Punic Wars. In 241 BC, after the First Punic War, Sicily became a Roman province, marking the beginning of Roman influence on the island. Roman rule brought stability and economic prosperity, with the cultivation of grain and the development of large estates or latifundia.

During the decline of the Western Roman Empire, Sicily experienced a series of invasions by Vandals, Ostrogoths, and Byzantines. The Byzantine Empire ultimately established control, and Sicily remained a Byzantine province for several centuries. The Arab-Muslim conquest in the 9th century introduced a new chapter in Sicily's history. Under Arab rule, the island witnessed a flourishing period of art, science, and agriculture. Palermo, the capital, became a center of Islamic culture and learning.

In the 11th century, the Normans, led by Roger I of Hauteville, embarked on the conquest of Sicily. This Norman rule was characterized by a unique blend of cultures, as the Normans embraced and incorporated elements of Arab and Byzantine traditions. The Norman Kingdom of Sicily reached its zenith under the rule of Roger II, who established a sophisticated court at Palermo and commissioned the construction of the famous Palatine Chapel, a testament to the multicultural influences on the island.

City View in Sicily, Italy

Following the Norman period, Sicily passed through the hands of various rulers, including the Hohenstaufens, Angevins, and Aragonese. The War of the Sicilian Vespers in the 13th century marked a pivotal moment, leading to the establishment of the Kingdom of Trinacria under Peter III of Aragon in 1282. The Trinacria, with its three-legged symbol, became an enduring emblem of Sicily.

The subsequent centuries saw the island's control shift between various European powers, including the Spanish Habsburgs and the House of Savoy. The Treaty of Utrecht in 1713 ceded Sicily to the Duchy of Savoy, and later, in 1720, it became a Bourbon possession. The Bourbons ruled Sicily until the unification of Italy in 1861.

Cefalù, Sicily

The Risorgimento, or Italian unification, brought significant changes to Sicily. Garibaldi's Expedition of the Thousand, a pivotal event in 1860, resulted in the annexation of Sicily to the Kingdom of Italy. The unification process, however, was not seamless, as the island faced economic challenges, social upheaval, and struggles for autonomy.

Sicily's role in World War II played a crucial part in the larger conflict. The Allied invasion of Sicily in 1943 marked the beginning of the end for Axis forces in Italy. The island became a crucial base for launching further Allied campaigns on the Italian mainland.

In the post-war period, Sicily underwent significant economic and social changes. The Mafia, a criminal organization deeply rooted in the island's history, gained notoriety for its influence on politics and society. Efforts to combat organized crime and promote economic development have been ongoing, shaping Sicily's contemporary landscape.

Today, Sicily stands as a testament to its diverse and complex history. The island's cultural heritage is reflected in its architecture, cuisine, and traditions. Visitors to Sicily encounter a mosaic of influences, from Greek temples and Roman amphitheaters to Arab-influenced architecture and Norman castles. The resilience and adaptability of the Sicilian people are evident in their ability to navigate a tumultuous history, shaping the unique identity of this captivating island in the heart of the Mediterranean.

Sicily Real Estate Market

Caption

Sicily, the largest island in the Mediterranean, is not only a historical and cultural gem but also a captivating destination for real estate enthusiasts. This comprehensive analysis delves into the intricacies of the real estate market in Sicily, exploring key trends, influencing factors, and the overall landscape for potential investors and stakeholders.

Market Overview

Sicily's real estate market is as diverse as the island itself, offering a range of properties from historic villas to seaside retreats. With a history influenced by various civilizations and a unique blend of landscapes, Sicily has become an attractive destination for those seeking a distinctive living experience. The market reflects this diversity, with opportunities ranging from urban investments to rural escapes.

Taormina, Sicily, Italy

Factors Influencing the Sicilian Market

Historical and Cultural Richness
Sicily's historical and cultural heritage is a significant driver of its real estate market. Properties with historical significance, such as palazzos and ancient estates, are in demand. Renovation projects that preserve the island's architectural legacy attract investors looking for a unique blend of history and modern living.

Seaside and Countryside Allure
The picturesque landscapes of Sicily, from golden beaches to rolling hills, contribute to the demand for properties along the coast and in the countryside. Seaside villas and rural estates appeal to those seeking tranquility and a connection with nature, creating distinct segments within the real estate market.

Tourism-Driven Opportunities
Sicily is a popular tourist destination, attracting visitors with it's ancient ruins, vibrant cities, and culinary delights. The tourism industry has created opportunities in the short-term rental market, especially in cities like Palermo and Taormina, where historic sites and cultural events draw international travelers.

Investment in Infrastructure
Ongoing and planned infrastructure projects, including improvements in transportation and connectivity, contribute to the overall attractiveness of Sicily's real estate. Enhanced accessibility makes remote and rural properties more appealing, fostering growth in areas previously considered secluded.

Revitalization Efforts and €1 Homes
Efforts to revitalize the Sicilian economy, including investments in agriculture, renewable energy, and cultural initiatives, play a role in shaping the real estate market. Areas experiencing economic growth often see increased demand for housing and commercial properties. Sicily has more towns participating in the €1 Home schemes than any other region in Italy. Many decades of population flight along with earthquakes and other factors have caused many areas of Sicily, mainly interior towns and villages, to lose large percentages of their populations. In an effort to reverse this trend, the local governments have begun reclaiming abondkanded homes and selling them for the symbolic price of €1.

Buyers should exercise caution with these purchases as they homes may need such extensive work that it would be cheaper to buy and existing home nearby that is move in ready, and skip the work and hassle required to bring a ruin back to life..

Taormina, Sicily, Italy

Current Market Dynamics

As of the latest data, Sicily's real estate market displays a mix of stability and dynamism. The demand for historical properties remains high, with Palermo, Catania, and Taormina serving as hotspots for urban investments. Seaside properties, especially in popular coastal towns like Cefalù and San Vito Lo Capo, continue to attract buyers seeking a Mediterranean lifestyle.

The short-term rental market, fueled by tourism, has experienced growth, with investors capitalizing on Sicily's popularity as a vacation destination. Additionally, rural properties, including renovated farmhouses and vineyard estates, have seen increased interest from both domestic and international buyers looking for a more secluded and authentic living experience.

Challenges and Risks

While Sicily's real estate market is promising, challenges exist. Zoning regulations, particularly in historic city centers, can pose obstacles to property development and renovation projects. Additionally, the economic disparities between different regions of Sicily may result in varying growth rates and investment opportunities.

Future Prospects

The future outlook for Sicily's real estate market is positive, driven by factors such as continued tourism growth, infrastructure development, and the island's overall appeal. However, stakeholders must navigate challenges related to sustainable development, regulatory frameworks, and economic disparities to ensure long-term success.

Sicily's real estate market presents a canvas painted with historical charm, cultural richness, and diverse landscapes. As the island continues to attract a mix of investors, from those seeking historical gems in urban centers to those yearning for tranquil rural retreats, strategic planning and a nuanced understanding of the market dynamics will be essential for unlocking Sicily's full real estate potential.

SARDINIA
Population: 1,628,000 (2018)

Cagliari, Sardinia, Italy

Sardinia, the second-largest island in the Mediterranean Sea, boasts a rich and varied history that spans thousands of years. Its story is marked by the influences of various civilizations, from ancient cultures to medieval kingdoms and modern nation-states.

The earliest known inhabitants of Sardinia were the Nuragic people, who left behind an impressive legacy of stone structures known as nuraghi. These megalithic towers, constructed between the Bronze Age and Iron Age, served various purposes, including defensive structures, religious sites, and residences. The nuragic civilization flourished for centuries, creating a distinctive cultural landscape that still captivates visitors to the island.

Bosa, Sardinia, Italy

In the 9th century BC, Phoenician and Carthaginian traders established settlements along Sardinia's coasts. Their influence introduced the island to the broader Mediterranean world and contributed to the island's economic and cultural development. However, Sardinia's strategic location also made it a target for various external powers, leading to periods of conquest and dominance.

Seaside, Sardinia, Italy

During the First Punic War in the 3rd century BC, Sardinia became a Roman province. Roman rule brought stability and infrastructure development, with the construction of roads, aqueducts, and cities. The ancient city of Caralis, modern-day Cagliari, became a thriving Roman hub. Sardinia's agricultural resources, particularly its grain production, played a crucial role in supporting the Roman Empire.

After the fall of the Western Roman Empire, Sardinia experienced a series of invasions and changes in rulership. The Vandals, Byzantines, and Arabs successively left their mark on the island. The Arab period, beginning in the 8th century, introduced Islam and Arab influence, leaving traces in Sardinia's language, architecture, and agriculture.

Castelsardo, Sardinia, Italy

The Byzantine Empire regained control of Sardinia in the 11th century, but the island faced continued incursions by various Mediterranean powers. The Pisans and the Genoese vied for dominance, leading to conflicts and power struggles. The maritime republics left behind architectural gems, including the Pisan Tower in Cagliari, that attest to their historical presence.
In the 14th century, the Crown of Aragon, under the rule of Alfonso IV, conquered Sardinia. The Aragonese period saw the establishment of a feudal system, with local nobility granted fiefdoms on the island. Sardinia became a part of the Kingdom of Aragon and later the Crown of Spain, solidifying its connection to the Iberian Peninsula.

Ocean View, Sardinia, Italy

The 18th century brought significant changes to Sardinia as the island became a battleground during the War of Spanish Succession. The Treaty of Utrecht in 1713 transferred Sardinia to the House of Savoy, marking the beginning of the Savoyard era. The Savoyards, later known as the Kings of Sardinia, established their capital in Cagliari, and the island became a crucial part of the expanding Savoyard state.

In the 19th century, Sardinia played a pivotal role in the unification of Italy. Count Camillo Benso di Cavour, the prime minister of the Kingdom of Sardinia, was a key figure in orchestrating the Risorgimento, the movement for Italian unification. Giuseppe Garibaldi's expedition of the Thousand, which aimed to liberate southern Italy and Sicily, began in

Sardinia, marking the island's contribution to the birth of modern Italy.

The late 19th and early 20th centuries witnessed social and economic transformations on the island. Sardinia, known for its mining industry, experienced industrialization and urbanization. However, the economic boom came with challenges, including labor strikes and social unrest. World War II brought its share of difficulties, with the island experiencing bombing raids and occupation by German and Italian forces.
After the war, Sardinia underwent a process of

Tower, Sardinia, Italy

reconstruction and development. The island's economy diversified, and tourism emerged as a significant industry, attracting visitors to its picturesque landscapes, archaeological sites, and pristine beaches. However, Sardinia also faced challenges related to environmental conservation and the preservation of its unique cultural heritage.

Today, Sardinia stands as an autonomous region of Italy, with a distinct identity shaped by its complex history. The island's archaeological sites, including the Nuragic complexes and Roman ruins, draw history enthusiasts and tourists alike. Sardinia's cultural richness is evident in its festivals, traditional cuisine, and the preservation of the Sardinian language. As the island continues to navigate the currents of history, it remains a fascinating and enduring testament to the diverse influences that have shaped its past.

Sardinia Real Estate Market

Sardinia, the second-largest island in the Mediterranean, is not only a haven of natural beauty but also a unique and enticing destination for real estate investment. This analysis delves into the intricacies of the real estate market in Sardinia, exploring key trends, influencing factors, and the overall landscape for potential investors and stakeholders.

Sardinia's real estate market is characterized by its diverse offerings, ranging from luxurious coastal properties to rustic countryside estates. The island's pristine beaches, rugged landscapes, and unique cultural identity contribute to the market's distinctive charm. Sardinia appeals to those seeking a blend of Mediterranean lifestyle, exclusivity, and natural splendor.

Current Trends in Sardinia

Coastal Luxury and Seaside Retreats
The allure of Sardinia's coastline, with its crystal-clear waters and hidden coves, attracts buyers seeking exclusive and luxurious properties. Seaside villas, often nestled in private enclaves, are in demand among high-net-worth individuals seeking a Mediterranean escape.

Countryside Retreats and Agrotourism
Sardinia's rugged interior, dotted with vineyards, olive groves, and traditional farmhouses, has sparked interest in countryside properties. The rise of agrotourism, where visitors experience rural life and local agriculture, has created opportunities for investors in this segment of the real estate market.

Cultural Preservation and Heritage Sites
Sardinia's rich cultural heritage, including ancient nuraghe towers and traditional festivals, influences the real estate market. Properties near heritage sites or within charming villages often attract those looking for a deeper connection with the island's history and traditions.

Global Appeal and International Investors
Sardinia has gained international recognition as a sought-after destination, drawing interest from global investors. The island's exclusive resorts and high-end properties appeal to a diverse range of buyers, including those from Northern Europe, Russia, and the Middle East.

Sustainable Tourism and Eco-friendly Development
The global emphasis on sustainable living has influenced Sardinia's real estate market. Eco-friendly developments and properties with a focus on sustainability and energy

efficiency are gaining popularity, aligning with the island's commitment to preserving its natural beauty.

Current Market Dynamics

As of the latest data, Sardinia's real estate market displays a dynamic interplay of demand across various segments. Coastal properties, particularly around the Costa Smeralda, remain a hotspot for luxury investments. Exclusive resorts, private villas, and waterfront estates are in high demand, attracting a discerning clientele seeking both prestige and privacy.

Countryside properties have seen increased interest, driven by a desire for tranquility and a slower pace of life. Agrotourism initiatives, where old farmhouses are transformed into charming accommodations, cater to those seeking an authentic Sardinian experience. The market reflects a balance between preserving the island's heritage and catering to modern luxury preferences.

Challenges and Risks

While Sardinia's real estate market presents lucrative opportunities, challenges exist. Striking a balance between development and environmental conservation is crucial, especially in ecologically sensitive areas. Zoning regulations and local opposition to large-scale projects can pose hurdles for investors, necessitating a nuanced approach to development.

Future Outlook

The future outlook for Sardinia's real estate market remains optimistic. The island's global appeal, commitment to sustainable development, and a diverse range of offerings position it as a resilient and attractive investment destination. Continued efforts to balance exclusivity with cultural preservation will be essential for long-term success.

In conclusion, Sardinia's real estate market is a mosaic of coastal opulence, rural charm, and cultural authenticity. As the island continues to captivate the imagination of investors and homebuyers alike, strategic planning, environmental stewardship, and a nuanced understanding of the market dynamics will be essential for unlocking Sardinia's full real estate potential..

FROSINONE
Population: 489,000 (2019)

Church in Acre, Frosinone Province

Frosinone, a province in the Lazio region of central Italy, has a history that spans thousands of years, reflecting the broader historical tapestry of the Italian peninsula. The province's rich heritage is marked by ancient civilizations, Roman influence, medieval dynamics, and the challenges of modernization.

The origins of Frosinone's settlement can be traced back to ancient times when the area was inhabited by the Volsci, an Italic people. The region's strategic location, nestled between the Tyrrhenian Sea and the central Apennine Mountains, made it a crossroads for trade and cultural exchange. The Volsci engaged in interactions with neighboring communities, leaving behind archaeological remnants that testify to their presence.

View in Frosinone Province, Italy

In the 4th century BC, the Roman Republic expanded its territory and influence over the Italian peninsula, bringing Frosinone under Roman rule. The area became part of the Roman administrative structure, with the development of roads and infrastructure contributing to the region's economic growth. The ancient Via Latina, an important Roman road, traversed the province, connecting Rome to the south of Italy.

During the Roman period, the town of Ferentino, now a major city in the province, flourished as a significant urban center. Roman ruins, including temples, baths, and amphitheaters, provide glimpses into Frosinone's ancient past. The agricultural landscape also thrived under Roman influence, contributing to the overall prosperity of the region.

With the decline of the Roman Empire in the 5th century, Frosinone, like much of Italy, experienced a period of instability and invasions. Germanic tribes, such as the Visigoths and Ostrogoths, as well as the Byzantines, successively controlled the region. The Lombards, a Germanic people, eventually established a more enduring presence in the 6th century.

The medieval period brought further changes to Frosinone as it became part of the Papal States, a collection of territories under the direct rule of the Pope. The Papal States aimed to assert control over central Italy and provide a buffer against external threats. Frosinone, situated on the eastern edge of the Papal States, became an important defensive outpost. The town of Anagni, another notable city in the province, gained prominence as a center of religious and political significance during this time.

In the 19th century, the political landscape of Frosinone underwent significant transformations with the unification of Italy, known as the Risorgimento. In 1870, Frosinone and the surrounding region were incorporated into the Kingdom of Italy. The province played a role in the struggles for Italian unification, with notable figures contributing to the cause.

The modernization and economic development of Frosinone accelerated in the 20th century. The agricultural sector continued to be vital to the region's economy, but industrialization and infrastructure projects, including the development of roads and railways, played a key role in shaping Frosinone's contemporary landscape. The city of Frosinone itself became an important industrial and commercial hub.

Roccasecca, Frosinone Province

In recent decades, Frosinone has faced challenges and opportunities associated with economic globalization and societal changes. The province has been part of initiatives to promote sustainable development and preserve its cultural heritage. Efforts to balance economic growth with

Steps in Arce, Italy

environmental conservation have become increasingly important.
Frosinone is known for its blend of historical sites, natural beauty, and modern amenities. Visitors to the province can explore ancient ruins, medieval towns, and picturesque landscapes. The region's cultural identity is reflected in its festivals, cuisine, and traditions, contributing to the overall charm of Frosinone as a dynamic and historically rich province in the heart of Italy.

Frosinone Real Estate Market

The Frosinone province consists of historic hilltop towns, some dating back over 2,000 years, and also flatland towns and cities that tend to be a bit newer and more modern as a whole. For the best views you want to be in the hilltop towns like Roccasecca, Arpino, Arce and so many dozens more... These towns have incredible deals on housing, often only €200-400/MQ ($20-40/sq ft). While the towns in the hills may not have all the services you want, everything is close at hand in the lower flatland towns just minutes away by car or bus.

While the area does get tourists, it is not heavily trafficked like Lucca or Florence. However, there are many pilgrims that traverse the area each year and there are numerous hotels and Bed and Breakfast's that cater to them and other tourists that find staying in the Frosinone area can be a rewarding experience.

Overall, homes and apartments in the Frosinone province are much less expensive than many areas of more northern areas in Italy. But this area has many things going for it like its proximity to Rome and even closer proximity to the beautiful beaches of southern Latina, another province in Lazio. You can easily drive 40 minutes from any of the hilltop towns in Frosinone and be on the beaches of Lazio. Likewise, a trip into the Rome city center is 90 minutes or less whether you're taking a train or a private automobile. This close proximity while still enjoying the low real estate cost make this province an incredible value in Italy.

Another great part of the Frosinone area is the well developed infrastructure. There are numerous large hospitals in the province and all services are close at hand.

Especially for those people that are in retirement years, you can't over emphasize the importance of having high-quality medical care close at hand. You wouldn't want to be an hour away from the nearest hospital and have a major concern come up.

Printed in Great Britain
by Amazon